SYSTEMS-CENTERED
THEORY AND PRACTICE

SYSTEMS-CENTERED THEORY AND PRACTICE
The Contribution
of Yvonne Agazarian

Presented by The Systems-Centered
Training and Research Institute and its
Board of Directors

Editorial Work Group
Fran Carter, Kathy Lum, Jim Peightel,
Michael Robbins, Michael Silverstein,
Jan Vadell and Sven-Erik Viskari

KARNAC

First published in 2010 by
WingSpan Press,
Livermore, CA, USA

This edition published in 2011 by
Karnac Books Ltd
118 Finchley Road
London NW3 5HT

Trademark Statements:
SCT® and Systems-Centered® are registered trademarks of Dr. Yvonne M. Agazarian and the Systems-Centered Training and Research Institute, Inc., a non-profit organization. SAVI® is a trademark of Anita Simon and Dr. Yvonne M. Agazarian.

Permissions:
Chapter Three, "Two Perspectives on a Trauma in a Training Group: The Systems-Centered Approach and the Theory of Incohesion" by Susan P. Gantt and Earl Hopper, is reproduced with permission of the authors. The complete article originally appeared in *Group Analysis* (2008) as a two-part series. [Gantt, S. P. & Hopper, E. (2008). Two perspectives on a trauma in a training group: The systems-centered approach and the theory of incohesion. Part I: *Group Analysis, 41*(1), 98–112. doi: 10.1177/0533316408088416. Part II: *Group Analysis, 41*(2), 123–139. doi: 10.1177/0533316408089879]

British Library Cataloguing in Publication Data

A C.I.P. for this book is available from the British Library

ISBN-13: 978-1-85575-747-9

Typeset by Vikatan Publishing Solutions (P) Ltd., Chennai, India

Printed in Great Britain

www.karnacbooks.com

CONTENTS

ACKNOWLEDGMENTS

The editorial group would like to acknowledge each of the contributors, Yvonne Agazarian, Ken Eisold, Susan Gantt, Earl Hopper, Christer Sandahl and Walter Stone, for their generosity and goodwill; the SCTRI Board of Directors for its vision and decision to create this monograph, and support of our work in implementing it; and most especially Yvonne Agazarian, for her leadership, wisdom and commitment in guiding and training us for so many years. The editorial group would also like to acknowledge the systems-centered methods that contained and supported the work of this group.

CONTRIBUTOR BIOGRAPHIES

Kenneth Eisold, Ph.D., a practicing psychoanalyst and organizational consultant, is a former president of the International Society for the Psychoanalytic Study of Organizations as well as former Director of the Organizational Program at The William Alanson White Institute, where he trains consultants in working psycho-dynamically with organizations. He is a Fellow of the A.K. Rice Institute. He has recently published a book on the unconscious, *What You Don't Know You Know*.

Susan P. Gantt, Ph.D., ABPP, CGP, FAGPA, FAPA, is a psychologist in private practice in Atlanta and Assistant Professor in Psychiatry at Emory University School of Medicine where she coordinates group psychotherapy training. She is the Director of the Systems-Centered Training and Research Institute. She is a Diplomate in Group Psychology through the American Board of Professional Psychology and co-author of the books *Autobiography of a Theory, SCT in Action* and *SCT in Clinical Practice* with Yvonne Agazarian. In private practice she works as a licensed SCT practitioner in systems-centered group, couples and individual therapy. She consults to organizations, and is a trainer, supervisor and conference director in systems-centered training in the U.S. and Europe.

Earl Hopper, Ph.D., MInstGA, CGP, is a psychoanalyst and group analyst in full time private practice. As a friend and colleague for 35 years, he is pleased to acknowledge Yvonne's important contributions to the field of group psychotherapy and group process. He is an Honorary Tutor at the Tavistock and Portman NHS Trust and a Member of the Post-Doctoral Program at Adelphi University, New York. He is the author of many books and articles on psychoanalysis, group analysis and sociology, and the Editor of *The New International Library of Group Analysis*.

Christer Sandahl, Ph.D., is a Professor of Social and Behavioral Sciences at the Medical Management Centre, Karolinska Institutet, Stockholm, Sweden. Together with his wife, Patricia Tudor Sandahl, he is the founder of Sandahl Partners Ltd., which now is a leading consultancy business within organizational psychology in Sweden. He is also a Past President of the International Association for Group Psychotherapy and Group Processes (IAGP).

Walter N. Stone, M.D., CGP, DFAGPA, is professor emeritus at the Department of Psychiatry of the University of Cincinnati and a Distinguished Fellow of the American Group Psychotherapy Association. His major clinical and research interest has been the application of Self Psychology to group psychotherapy and to the treatment of the persistent and seriously mentally ill. In retirement, he continues to volunteer and teach at several sites in Northern California. He is the co-author of *Psychodynamic Group Psychotherapy* and the author of three books and more than 50 articles and book chapters.

BIOGRAPHY

Yvonne M. Agazarian, Ed.D, CGP, DFAGPA, FAPA, is the developer of the Theory of Living Human Systems and its Systems-Centered practice, founder of the Systems-Centered Training and Research Institute, and facilitator in the development of systems-centered training centers in Atlanta, Austin, Boston, New York, Philadelphia, and San Francisco as well as in London, York and Stockholm. She consults, teaches and trains in the systems-centered method internationally. She is a Clinical Professor at Adelphi University and is in private practice for group and individual therapy in Philadelphia. In addition to many articles, she is the author of *Systems-Centered Therapy for Groups* (1997), *A Systems-Centered Approach to Inpatient Group Psychotherapy* (2001), and *Systems-Centered Practice: Selected Papers on Group Psychotherapy* (2006). She co-authored *The Visible and Invisible Group* with Richard Peters (1981), and *Autobiography of a Theory* with Susan Gantt (2000). Also with Susan Gantt, Yvonne co-edited the books *SCT in Action: Applying the Systems-Centered Approach in Organizations* (2005), and *SCT in Clinical Practice: Applying the Systems-Centered Approach with Individuals, Families and Groups* (2006).

Her proudest moment was in 1997 when she received the Group Psychologist of the Year award from Division 49 of the American Psychological Association, *"For her involvement in research, publication, teaching and training. She exemplifies the finest in scholarship in the discipline of psychology. As a group psychologist, she has contributed to expanding our knowledge of the boundaries between clinical and social psychology with the investigation of living human systems and systems-centered group and individual therapy. Her considerable body of work illustrates the highest blend of creativity and learning"*.

Curriculum Vitae

Education

1963–1968	Ed.D., Group Dynamics, Department of Educational Psychology, Temple University, Philadelphia, PA
1960–1963	P.S.A., Psychoanalysis, Certificate: Psychoanalytic Studies Institute, Philadelphia, PA
1961–1962	M.Ed., Group Dynamics, Group Dynamics Center, Temple University, Philadelphia, PA
1948–1952	B.A., English and Philosophy, University of British Columbia, Vancouver, Canada

Postgraduate training and fellowship appointments

1962–1965	Teaching Fellow, Temple University, Department of Group Dynamics and Educational Psychology, Philadelphia, PA

Faculty appointments

1999–current	Clinical Professor, Adelphi Post-Doctoral Program in Group Psychotherapy, New York
1990–2005	Consulting Affiliate: Friends Hospital, Philadelphia, PA
1986–1998	Annual Organizational Development and Staff Training, Gentofte Hospital, Copenhagen, Denmark
1990–1992	University of Pennsylvania, Research Program into Short-Term Psychotherapy, Philadelphia, PA
1988–1991	Clinical Associate of the Center for Short-Term Dynamic Psychotherapy at St. Claire's Hospital, New Jersey
1978–1988	Clinical Assistant Professor, Hahnemann Medical College, Philadelphia, PA
1968–1970	Supervisor, Group Psychotherapy, Residency Training Program, Institute of Pennsylvania Hospital, Philadelphia, PA

Current positions

1962–current   Private Practice, Philadelphia, PA
1991–current   Teaching, training and treating in Systems-centered
               approach to individual and group therapy and
               organizational consultation. Developer of the Theory
               of Living Human Systems. Founder of the Systems-
               Centered Training and Research Institute.

Previous positions

1995–2002   Director, Systems-Centered Training and Research
            Institute, Philadelphia, PA
1970–1972   Director of Residency Group Training, Philadelphia
            Mental Health Clinic, Philadelphia, PA
1965–1970   Director of Outpatient Group Psychotherapy,
            Community Mental Health Center, Pennsylvania
            Hospital, Philadelphia, PA

The achievements and influence of Yvonne Agazarian

Susan P. Gantt, Ph.D., ABPP, CGP, FAGPA, FAPA

This monograph is presented by the Systems-Centered Training and Research Institute (SCTRI) on the occasion of Yvonne Agazarian's 80th birthday in honor and appreciation of the contributions she has made with her theory of living human systems and its systems-centered practice, the founding of SCTRI, and in training and mentoring so many of us.

I am enormously pleased in my role as Director of SCTRI to be writing this brief overview of Yvonne's many contributions as theoretician, clinician, consultant, and founder and director emeritus of SCTRI. I am also pleased personally to be writing this as Yvonne has impacted me and my work deeply.

In this brief introduction, I hope to convey some of the highlights of Yvonne's contributions in developing a systems theory that can be applied with all living human systems, whether individual people, couples, families, organizational work groups, organizations, or even nations.

Taking to heart the task of applying systems thinking to group psychotherapy

As an earnest graduate student in the 1960's, Yvonne was appalled at the difficulty crossing between the language and constructs of individual psychoanalytic psychotherapy and those of group dynamics. Dave Jenkins, her professor at Temple, suggested to her she formulate a theory that would integrate both. This was the beginning impetus for what was much later to become a theory of living human systems. Another major catalyst began in 1980 when Yvonne joined the American Group Psychotherapy Association's (AGPA) General Systems Theory (GST) committee chaired by Helen Durkin. When this committee disbanded ten years later, Yvonne took to heart Jay Fiddler's personally urging her to apply GST to the practice of group psychotherapy. Jay's charge stayed with Yvonne much as the project Dave Jenkins had proposed. By the early 1990's, Yvonne's theory of living human systems was rapidly taking shape and she articulated both the theory and practice in her 1997 book, *Systems-Centered Therapy for Groups* (Agazarian, 1997). This text still today remains the handbook for systems-centered training (SCT).

A theory of living human systems

Yvonne's theory of living human systems offers the most coherent and well-developed systems theory in its application to psychotherapy yet formulated. She describes it as a meta-theory in that a theory of living human systems can be used to understand and frame any method of change. Her theory of living human systems defines a "hierarchy of isomorphic systems that are energy-organizing, goal-directed and system-correcting" (Agazarian, 1997). Beginning with this one sentence statement of the theory, Yvonne then defined each of the constructs: hierarchy and isomorphy. Making definitions at each level of abstraction led to creating operational definitions from which hypotheses were derived and from which the methods and techniques of systems-centered training were then developed. As Yvonne says, each technique then tests the validity of the theory and the reliability of its practice. (Chapter one, Series V in this monograph is Yvonne's Friends' Series paper that elaborates her theory "Building Blocks of a Theory of Living Human Systems and its Systems-Centered Practice".) For example, hierarchy defines that a system always exists in the context of the system above it and is the context for the system below it in the hierarchy. In applying this idea, Yvonne recognized the enormous implications of always seeing a system or a subsystem in its context, that is, a system is never in isolation, it always exists in a context. Today SCT practitioners work actively with the understanding that whenever we take ourselves just personally, we have lost awareness of our context. Isomorphy is defined as similarity in structure and function for systems in a defined hierarchy. Structure is then operationally defined as boundaries that are permeable or impermeable to the flow of energy and information. Function is defined as the process by which living human systems survive, develop and transform from simpler to more complex through the process of discriminating and integrating differences, both differences in the apparently similar and similarities in the apparently different. Making this definition of function operational led to developing the method of functional subgrouping. Functional subgrouping is quite possibly the contribution that has had the most impact on the field of group therapy and arguably may be the most influential and longest lasting of Yvonne's many contributions.

Functional subgrouping

Functional subgrouping is the heart of SCT practice. In fact, without functional subgrouping, a group is not an SCT group. Yvonne's introduction of the method of functional subgrouping as a conflict resolution method has gained wide acceptance from not only SCT practitioners but also from a broad theoretical array of practitioners, many of whom have integrated functional subgrouping into their practice. Many have recognized the enormous impact functional subgrouping has on weakening the acting-out of scapegoating. Yvonne developed the method of functional subgrouping from her theory and her keen observations of groups that enabled her to discriminate functional from stereotyped or "basic assumptions" (Bion, 1959) subgrouping. To reiterate, the theory behind functional subgrouping is simple and profound: to the extent that a living human system discriminates and integrates its differences, it will survive, develop and transform. Functional subgrouping is a method that enables this process of discriminating differences in the apparently similar and similarities in the apparently different. In practice, any time there is a difference that is experienced as "too different", members choose which side of the conflict to explore in a subgroup with others who are also resonant with this side, and then in turn the second subgroup explores the other side of the conflict they are holding until there is an integration in the group-as-a-whole. Or, whenever someone says "yes, but", they are offered the option of exploring either the "yes" or the "but", and encouraged to find out who else wants to explore their chosen side with them by asking "anyone else?" (One of Yvonne's early papers on functional subgrouping is included in Chapter 1, Series I of this monograph, entitled "Functional Subgrouping". Also Yvonne's book, *A Systems-Centered Approach to Inpatient Group Psychotherapy*, published in 2001, provides an actual transcript of Yvonne working with a group and illustrates functional subgrouping.) Applying functional subgrouping to both therapy groups and training groups has enabled them to contain and explore group conflicts and the underlying group dynamics rather than acting them out by creating identified patients or scapegoats.

Driving and restraining forces in the phases of system development

Another major contribution is Yvonne's formulation of her phases of system development. Building on Bion (1959) and Bennis and Shepard's (1956) translation of Bion into a theory of group development, Yvonne applied the ideas of phases of development to systems and then integrated these phases of system development with Lewin's force field (1951). This enabled Yvonne to identify a predictable force field for each phase of system development, which then provided a map for change interventions. As Lewin would say, weakening the restraining forces releases the inherent drive to the goal. Weakening the restraining forces relevant to the system's phase of development then releases the driving forces toward development. For clinical practice, Yvonne then used this theoretical map to develop a hierarchy of defense modifications linked to the phases of systems development, enabling therapists to tie their interventions to the context of the phase of the system's development.

This hierarchy then guides a therapist in the process of change, and more easily enables a modular approach to therapy when the reality constraints dictate short-term therapies.

The construct of role and moving from person to member

From early in her theorizing, Yvonne has worked with the construct of role as a bridge construct between the individual and the group. She introduced this idea in her first book, *The Visible and Invisible Group*, that she co-authored with her co-therapist Richard Peters in 1981. Later, using systems theory, Yvonne discriminated between the system of a person, which provides the energy for all living human systems, and the system of a member, which is the role that we take to relate to the goal of the context. Member role is the intervening subsystem between the person and the context. Most significantly, the first challenge is learning to take membership in one's self; learning to weaken the restraining forces or encapsulated internal roles that inhibit us from being more of ourselves. The next ongoing challenge is bringing our person system into our member role so that we can take up our roles in all the systems in which we are members with our heart and personal energy. Learning to take membership also weakens the human tendency to personalize that not only causes us anguish but also inhibits us from bringing our energy into the system and contributing to the group. As Yvonne says, learning to take things not "just personally" lowers the anguish for human beings. Similarly, learning to see the role, goal and context always lowers our human tendency to personalize.

Yvonne introduced the model of role, goal and context that is central in applying SCT to organizations. Learning to orient to the goal of the system context is critical in knowing how to take one's role to support the goal of one's context. This same model guides SCT practitioners in their work with couples, in which this model is introduced to the couple in terms of the four subsystems in a marriage, each of which has a goal and roles that implement the goal. For example, the parenting subsystem has the goal of raising children into functional adults, or as Yvonne often puts it: "importing babies and exporting adults". The roles in this context are mother and father. Many marital conflicts are resolved when the couple understands that they are relating from incompatible role systems, e.g., when one responds from the role of intimacy and the other from the parenting role of bathing the baby. Starting couples work with the clarity of these functional roles has enabled an important platform for the later work with the habitual roles that lock couples into redundant and dysfunctional patterns.

System for Analyzing Verbal Interaction (SAVI)

In the 1960's prior to developing SCT, Yvonne and her good friend Anita Simon developed SAVI, a coding system for observing and coding verbal interactions. The theory behind SAVI drew from Shannon and Weaver's (1964) mathematical theory of communication that postulated an inverse relationship between noise in the communication channel and the probability that the information in the channel would be received. Yvonne also drew from Howard and Scott's theory of stress (1965) which viewed all behavior as approaching or avoiding conflicts on the path to the goal and Lewin's (1951) force field in looking at the relationship between the verbal behaviors that approached the goal of the transfer of information, and the restraining forces that avoided it. The SAVI system enables categorization of verbal communications into a frequency matrix that identifies communication patterns in a system, and the likelihood of these patterns moving the system toward or away from successful communication, i.e., the transfer of information. SAVI enabled a focus on "how" something is said, not "what" is said, by identifying verbal behaviors that are restraining forces (like ambiguity, redundancy or contradictory talk) that make it difficult to hear "what" is said. SAVI and its theory not only provided a viable tool for training in effective communication and a research tool for learning to observe a system's communication patterns, but also laid a foundation for the later development of SCT and its theory of living human systems. In a research project some years ago, Yvonne used SAVI to code communications in a therapy group and identified a fligt pattern. flight pattern. Each time an individual would deviate from the flight norm, the group pattern would return to the norm. Most telling of the power of the system pattern was the moment in the group where there were 3–4 consecutive group communications that moved out of flight and the therapist's communication put the group back into flight. From this analysis Yvonne became convinced that it is the group communication pattern that determines the problem-solving potential in the group, not the individuals, however skilled the individuals are.

High on integrating

In all of her contributions, which are far greater than this brief summary allows, Yvonne's brilliance in integrating knowledge and other theories has enabled her to develop her highly integrative theory and systems-centered practice. To this day, Yvonne continues in this work as she is actively integrating research from interpersonal neurobiology into the systems-centered practice. This ongoing effort points to the heart of SCT. It is not a static theory or practice, but is always developing and emerging. And though Yvonne's major focus is clinical and organizational development, many others that she has trained have imported the work into education, professional coaching, and managerial and leadership training.

SCTRI

One other contribution is important to note. In 1995, Yvonne implemented her vision and founded SCTRI, a non-profit organization. Developing this organization built on workshops Yvonne had held at Friends Hospital in Philadelphia as well as in Boston, Austin, and the University of York, and ongoing New York and Philadelphia training groups she had been leading. In fact, Yvonne had introduced the idea of becoming an organization in the debriefing period following a Philadelphia workshop. There were immediately two subgroups, one excited about "organizing" and the other more reluctant and determined to organize without any hierarchy! Yvonne, working closely with three friends and colleagues, Claudia Byram, Fran Carter, and Anita Simon, used the theory and practice of SCT to build and develop SCTRI, that is, putting SCT into organizational practice. These four took the leadership in exploring how to make the theory practical, in designing training curriculum and experiences for an ever-widening interest. They were determined not to replicate traditional organizations, and instead followed the idea of "laying the paths by following where the members trod" so that structure did not dominate function and emergence. This experiment has led to an active international organization of 230 members, many of whom are in SCT training in one of the 12 training groups in the US or one of the four in Europe and who subgroup by telephone to do the work of the organization. Many of these members also gather once a year for the SCT annual conference, which just celebrated its tenth anniversary. SCTRI has recently been presented the 2010 Award for Outstanding Contributions in Education and Training in the Field of Group Psychotherapy given by the National Registry of Certified Group Psychotherapists, the credentialing arm of the American Group Psychotherapy Association.

Courage to bring in differences

Along the way of developing her theory, Yvonne has provided an important model by having the courage to say what she knows and to speak the unspeakable. Two episodes illustrate this well. In 1989, Yvonne was an invited discussant for Harold Sampson and Joseph Weiss who were invited lecturers for the Slavson Memorial Lecture at AGPA (Agazarian, 1989a; Agazarian & Gantt, 2000). In preparing her remarks, Yvonne linked her systems theory to Sampson and Weiss' idea of the pathogenic belief, toward the goal of generalizing their work to group dynamics. In doing this, Yvonne recognized the pathogenic belief inherent in psychoanalysis and individual therapy, that the first pathogenic belief is that the patient is the center of the world, which masks a deeper pathogenic belief that the analyst is the center of the world. Having trained as a psychoanalyst, this recognition seemed heresy to Yvonne as she recognized that therapy can actually encourage self-centeredness at the expense of seeing the larger system context. Yet she held fast to what she had seen as she described in her remarks how group therapy can weaken the pain that comes from an "egocentric focus".

Or similarly, when on a panel with Irvin Yalom in 1992 at AGPA where excerpts of his tapes were shown and discussed, Yvonne used "who to whom", which tracks who is speaking to whom, and SAVI to code the communication patterns in the group excerpts (Agazarian, 1992; Agazarian & Gantt, 2000). In both excerpts, the pattern was "communication to a deviant". In the first, the group elected an identified patient for the therapist to cure, and in the second, a scapegoat for the group to blame. Yvonne then described how a systems-centered approach would differ, by encouraging functional subgrouping to explore the roles that were being enacted.

Both of these experiences are described in *Autobiography of a Theory*, which Yvonne and I co-authored. In this book, Yvonne traces the steps along the way to developing her theory and the moments and influences in her life that contributed to her work.

Yvonne's favorite of her books, *Systems-Centered Practice: Selected Papers on Group Psychotherapy* (2006), brings together published articles from 1987–2002 that illustrate Yvonne's theory and the stepping stones in her thinking as she is developing it. In fact, her own summary of this book describes the theoretical challenge to which she has devoted her work: "The book covers various stages in my attempts to solve the problem represented by the fact that, though group dynamics are different from the dynamics of individuals, group is often defined as the sum of individual dynamics" (Agazarian, 2006, p. 1).

Recognition

As Yvonne's theory strongly emphasizes, the challenge of introducing a difference is not easy as human beings tend to close their boundaries to differences that are too different. And SCT does introduce radical differences. It is a tribute to the clarity of Yvonne's theorizing and apprehensive understandings that, in spite of the radical differences she has introduced, she has gained wide recognition. For example, she was invited to deliver the 12th Annual Foulkes Memorial Lecture in 1989, was recognized as a Fellow in the American Psychological Association, and has been named a Distinguished Fellow in the American Group Psychotherapy Association. She also served for ten years on the board of the International Association of Group Psychotherapy and for eight years as the first Director of the Systems-Centered Training and Research Institute. There have been many highlights in Yvonne's prolific contributions and many significant moments, but none more telling than her recognition as Group Psychologist of the Year in 1997 by Division 49 of the American Psychological Association:

> *"For her involvement in research, publication, teaching and training. She exemplifies the finest in scholarship in the discipline of psychology. As a group psychologist, she has contributed to expanding our knowledge of the boundaries between clinical and social psychology*

with the investigation of living human systems and systems-centered group and individual therapy. Her considerable body of work illustrates the highest blend of creativity and learning."

Yvonne's influence is far reaching. As a group theorist and practitioner, few have offered the coherent theory and practice that she has developed and introduced, the training program that she pioneered, the training and research institute that she founded, and the books and articles she has authored. Just as important to Yvonne are the thousands that she has trained directly and the even larger number who have read her many books and articles world-wide. It is also valuable to note the strong personal connections she forms with those she teaches and trains: some may think this paradoxical as Yvonne has so strongly emphasized the system and the importance of learning to shift from person to member and take membership in one's person. Yet it is the resources of us as people that are the energy and life force in living human systems and as those who know Yvonne well know, the person energy is the life force for any living human system.

For myself, from my first experience with Yvonne in the early 1990's at an AGPA meeting in San Antonio, where I learned to work with the group rather than struggle internally with myself, I recognized that Yvonne offered a theory and method that are unique and revolutionary. Yvonne has been the most significant mentor I have had and my personal and professional association with her ranks as the most influential of my life, and most importantly, there are many others who would say this as well. For Yvonne lives as she teaches, and builds the relational system with whomever she is relating. This may be her greater legacy to us all, to take up the call of membership and citizenship wherever we are, albeit with ourselves, our loved ones, our colleagues, our organizations, our countries and our world.

The articles in this monograph

This monograph starts with a series of papers used in the Friends Hospital training that Yvonne selected to include here. These five previously unpublished papers are followed by four other papers, contributed by leaders in different aspects of the clinical and organizational fields, all of whom contributed to honor Yvonne, as they address and dialogue with Yvonne's ideas, contributions and influence.

1. **Five Papers from the Friends Hospital Training Series: Fall 1992 to Fall 1995** *by Yvonne Agazarian.* These five papers introduced systems-centered therapy and training at Friends Hospital, between 1992 and 1995, and cover the essential aspects of systems-centered training. The five papers are:

   I. "Functional Subgrouping" provides both the theory and method of functional subgrouping;
   II. "How to Develop a Working Group". Here Yvonne describes boundaries as the difference that makes a difference, and discusses both the importance of boundaries to contain group energy and clear goals for direction;
   III. "Defense Modification" summarizes the early version of Yvonne's defense modification for modifying social defenses, boundary defenses, role lock defenses, and transforming defenses and the importance of undoing defenses to regain primary experiences;
   IV. "Subgrouping in the Phases of Group Development" describes the phases of a systems-centered group that provide the context for development that, when influenced in the group, will also influence the subgroup and the members. This then means that the work of therapy is done in the process of building the group system;
   V. "Building Blocks of a Theory of Living Human Systems and its Systems-Centered Practice". Here Yvonne summarizes her theory and the operational definitions that put it into practice.

2. **The Radical Innovation of Subgroups** *by Ken Eisold.* Ken Eisold presents a strong recognition of Yvonne's radical innovations, especially how Yvonne's work and method of functional subgrouping enable a shift in group therapy away from enacting the cultural belief that we are the center of the world. He describes his perspective on her contributions of functional subgrouping, energy and role and his appreciation of how she has avoided the typical Newtonian assumptions in her theorizing. He summarizes her work from his perspective as a group relations leader

and psychoanalyst and puts it into context by relating it to the challenges psychoanalytic theorists and others have faced. Most importantly, he reminds us that indeed Yvonne's radical work enables us to "go beyond who we thought we were".

3. **Two Perspectives on a Trauma in a Training Group: The Systems-Centered Approach and the Theory of Incohesion** *by Susan P. Gantt and Earl Hopper.* This paper describes an SCT training group that was observed by Earl Hopper through a collaboration among Earl, Yvonne and Susan Gantt. Inadvertently, the group was traumatized as the leader neglected to let the group know about the observation. Using the group's interrupted session as the focus, the article presents a dialogue between the systems-centered approach and Earl Hopper's theory of incohesion. This important interchange not only describes Yvonne's theory in practice with a group trauma but also discusses the differences as well as the strong similarities in understanding in the two approaches.

4. **Role, Goal and Context: Key Issues for Group Therapists and Group Leaders** *by Christer Sandahl.* In this paper, Christer Sandahl recognizes the importance Yvonne's friendship and professional influence have had on his work. He takes the ideas of role, goal and context, a model developed by Yvonne in SCT practice, and links it to the work of another major influence on his work, Bruce Reed and his work on role. Christer then describes his applications with leadership, context and role, influenced and supported by both Yvonne and Bruce, who he describes as his "professional parents".

5. **SCT Applications to Psychodynamic Group Psychotherapy** *by Walter N. Stone.* Walter Stone compares SCT to psychodynamic group therapy and presents a description of a psychodynamic demonstration group that he led at an SCT conference. Using this example, he discusses the systems-centered viewpoint and contrasts this with his self-psychology perspective, noting both parallel paths and ways that SCT diverges, especially in the therapist's role. Walt also offers an overview of the SCT technique of the "fork-in-the-road" and compares it to Kohut's two-part interpretive process, again exploring the similarities and

differences. He ends by highlighting both his appreciation and perspective in seeing Yvonne's theory develop over his 30 year friendship with her.

References

Agazarian, Y. M. (1989a, February). *Pathogenic beliefs and implicit goals: Discussion of "The Mount Zion group: The therapeutic process and applicability of the group's work to psychotherapy"*. Paper presented at the Slavson Memorial Lecture, American Group Psychotherapy Association Annual Meeting, San Francisco.

Agazarian, Y. M. (1989b). The invisible group: An integrational theory of group-as-a-whole. The 12th Annual Foulkes Memorial Lecture. *Group Analysis, 22*(4), 74–96.

Agazarian, Y. M. (1992, February). *The use of two observation systems to analyze the communication patterns in two videotapes of the interpersonal approach to group psychotherapy.* [Based on I. D. Yalom "Understanding group psychotherapy" (videotape). Pacific Grove, CA: Brooks-Cole.] Panel on "Contrasting views of representative group events", American Group Psychotherapy Association Annual Meeting, New Orleans.

Agazarian, Y. M. (1997). *Systems-centered therapy for groups.* New York: Guilford Press. Re-printed in paperback (2004). London: Karnac Books.

Agazarian, Y. M. (2001). *A systems-centered approach to inpatient group psychotherapy.* London and Philadelphia: Jessica Kingsley.

Agazarian, Y. M. (2006). *Systems-centered practice: Selected papers on group psychotherapy.* London: Karnac Books.

Agazarian, Y. M. (1995/2010). Five papers from the Friends Hospital training series: Fall 1992–Fall 1995. In Carter, F. Lum, K. Peightel, J. Robbins, M. Silverstein, M. Vadell, J. Viskari, S. E. (Eds.), *Systems-centered theory and practice: The contribution of Yvonne Agazarian* (pp. 1–46). Livermore, CA: WingSpan Press. (Previously unpublished papers)

Agazarian, Y. M. & Gantt, S. P. (2000). *Autobiography of a theory.* London: Jessica Kingsley.

Agazarian, Y. M. & Peters, R. (1981). *The visible and invisible group.* London: Routledge & Kegan Paul, Ltd. Re-printed in paperback (1987). London: Karnac Books.

Bennis, W. G. & Shepard, H. A. (1956). A theory of group development. *Human Relations, 9*(4), 415–437.

Bion, W. R. (1959). *Experiences in groups*. London: Tavistock.

Howard, A. & Scott, R. A. (1965). A proposed framework for the analysis of stress in the human organism. *Journal of Applied Behavioral Science, 10,* 141–160.

Lewin, K. (1951). *Field theory in social science*. New York: Harper & Row.

Shannon, C. E. & Weaver, W. (1964). *The mathematical theory of communication*. Urbana, IL: University of Illinois Press.

CHAPTER ONE

Five papers from the Friends Hospital training series: Fall 1992 to Fall 1995

Yvonne Agazarian, Ed.D., CGP, DFAGPA, FAPA

T hese are the original papers from the "Friends Series", a training that was held once a month on Saturdays at the Friends Hospital in Philadelphia, Pennsylvania. The series began in the early 1990's and continued through the decade with two generations of trainers taking up leadership roles. These papers represent some of the earliest descriptions of SCT methods and theory. The theoretical thinking and techniques that emerged during that period continue to be the backbone of the Theory of Living Human Systems and its Systems-Centered practice today.

These five papers were the first introduction to Systems-centered Therapy and Training at Friends Hospital, between 1992 and 1995. The five papers are: I: Functional Subgrouping, II: How to Develop a Working Group, III: Defense Modification, IV: Subgrouping in the Phases of Group Development, V: Building Blocks of a Theory of Living Human Systems and its Systems-Centered Practice.

* * *

Series I: functional subgrouping

> Asking *"why are you saying that?"*
> or *"tell me more about that!"*
> is like giving another member's boat
> a push out to sea.
>
> Saying *"I'm in your subgroup"*
> is like an encouraging wave from the shore.
>
> Working as a member of your subgroup is more than
> pushing another member's boat out to sea,
> or waving encouragingly from the shore.
>
> Subgrouping is getting into the boat
> and rowing too!

The **subgroup,** not the individual member, is the basic unit of the systems-centered group. Not the obvious stereotype subgroups, like age or sex or race, but functional subgroups. All subgroups naturally come together around similarities and separate around differences. Functional subgroups are different from stereotypic subgroups in that functional subgroups come together around *dynamic differences,* thus mirroring the way that systems develop. All systems differentiate and individuate through a process of integrating ever more complex discriminations: discriminating differences in the apparently similar and similarities in the apparently different.

Once subgroups are "seen" as systems, the therapist can deliberately influence subgroup dynamics in the service of containing and integrating group splits which occur naturally around differences. In systems-centered therapy, the subgroup is the fulcrum of change and there are some specific techniques for mastering developmental conflicts in the group through functional subgrouping. Explicitly encouraging the group to do subgroup work interrupts the spontaneous fight/flight response to differences and replaces it with the discipline of "functional subgrouping" (Agazarian, 1991).

Functional subgrouping

Systems-centered therapy is the method by which the therapist encourages the group to learn the skills of how to communicate within and between subgroups. When similarities and differences are processed within and between subgroups, integration takes place at the group-as-a-whole level.

"The automatic response to difference is defensive and conflicted. Groups tend to split the 'similar enough and good' from the 'too different and bad': take in the 'good,' reject the 'bad'". (Agazarian, 1992). Functional subgrouping exploits the natural developmental process of system splitting and containing. Systems-centered therapy relies on the technique of functional subgrouping to contain splits, metabolize projective identifications and to overcome the compulsion to repeat that is generic to every individual. The technique of functional subgrouping is also the method by which phases of group development are influenced: resistances to change weakened, and the forces that drive the system towards its goals of survival, development and environmental mastery are increased.

Traditionally, in the group-as-a-whole, the first subgroups to appear represent the obvious and most simple "containment" of differences in a group, like sex, age, color, race, and status. Stereotype subgrouping is one of the first ways the group-as-a-whole structures itself to contain its differences and maintain group stability. Later in dynamic development, the group-as-a-whole uses the roles of "benevolent leader", "malevolent leader", "the scapegoat" and the "identified patient" as containers for its un-integrated splits around differences. This dynamic is so dramatic in group development, that the less obvious dynamic of "functional subgrouping" can go unnoticed in the developmental process. Stereotype subgrouping is the simplest level of functional subgrouping (Agazarian, 1990b). Subgroups naturally come together around similarities and separate around differences, thus mirroring the developmental process of discriminating and integrating. Thus the dynamic that underlies the function of subgrouping, mirrors the dynamics of system development and can be deliberately harnessed in the service of containing and integrating group splits. Explicitly encouraging the group to do subgroup work interrupts the spontaneous fight response to differences and replaces it with the discipline of "functional subgrouping".

The most efficient method for facilitating the subgroup work of discrimination and integration is to encourage the exploration of experience within each individual subgroup before there is any cross-subgroup communication. Thus, by the very process of development, the internal process shifts from the cohesion around similarities to seeing differences in the cohesively similar. This process increases differentiation within each subgroup and increases the permeability potential of the boundaries between the subgroups. When boundaries become appropriately permeable to a transfer of information, similarities between the differing subgroups are perceived and new subgroups can form. This is the process of system integration and the ongoing task of crossing from irreality to reality (and from the unconscious to the preconscious to the conscious).

Some functional subgroups appear as obviously balanced dichotomies in the group that the leader can easily encourage the group to explore: cognition and affect; compliance and defiance; closeness and distance. Others are less obvious and have to be "believed" before they are seen: like seeing that fighting members belong to the same subgroup and are one of two group subgroups balancing the groups' fight and flight response. When the systems-centered therapist manages conflict through functional subgrouping, the group is encouraged to first identify and then to "take sides" in the conflict, and to do their individual insight work in the supported context of the subgroup. This bypasses ambivalence: the common defense against the experience of being pulled two ways by the forces of both sides of the conflict. The therapist encourages a conscious splitting into subgroups and, by so doing, discourages defensive splitting within individuals. The conflict is **contained** within the group-as-a-whole rather than within each individual. Through membership in a subgroup, individuals are supported in their work of exploring one single side of their version of the conflict instead of denying, projecting or acting out in the struggle to contain both at once.

By promoting functional subgrouping, the "container" roles (like the scapegoat or the identified patient) that are created through projective identification are addressed, not by focusing on the individual who takes up the role, but in terms of the subgroup that the individual represents, and the role that the subgroup is playing for the group-as-a-whole. In this way, reintegrating projected differences becomes the explicit work of the group-as-a-whole rather than the "problem" of the individual or the subgroup.

The difference between functional subgroups and stereotype subgroups

Functional subgroups	Stereotype subgroups
all subgroups join around similarities and split around differences	all subgroups join around similarities and split around differences
functional subgroups contain and explore differences instead of stereotyping and scapegoating them	stereotype subgroups come together around obvious similarities like black and white, male and female, them and us
functional subgroups join around similarities and split differences between them	everybody knows how to make stereotype subgroups
functional subgroups "contain" all conflict within the group-as-a-whole	everybody knows what to do and what to say to make top dogs, under dogs and little dogs
as each subgroup discovers new differences by exploring the similarities within them so each subgroup discovers new similarities by exploring the differences between them	everybody knows how to keep the ups up and the downs down
when the differences within each subgroup join with the similarities between each subgroup the group-as-a-whole transforms into a new group able to work differently from the old group	everybody knows how to keep the ins in and the outs out
	everybody knows how to make scapegoats of each other
	stereotype subgrouping discriminates differences and won't integrate them
re-integrating around similarities after deliberately splitting around differences moves the group-as-a-whole along the path to its goal	stereotype subgrouping manages the hatred and fear that is aroused by differences by creating a social pecking order
functional subgrouping upsets the social order by making a place for everyone and letting everyone find their place to make the social system work	by having a place for everyone and keeping everyone in their place stereotype subgrouping keeps the social system stable

Through membership in a subgroup, individual members are supported in their work of exploring one single side of their version of the conflict instead of denying, projecting or acting out in the struggle to contain both at once. When the systems-centered therapist manages conflict through functional subgrouping, members are encouraged to first identify and then to "take sides" in the conflict, and to do their individual insight work in the supportive context of the subgroup. This bypasses ambivalence, the common defense against the *experience* of being pulled two ways. By subgrouping functionally around the two sides of a conflict, defensive splitting is changed into a conscious split in the service of work. Every individual always belongs in more than one subgroup at once, but no individual can *work* in more than one subgroup at once. By deliberately choosing to subgroup, the conflict is deliberately split between subgroups. In this way, the conflict is **contained** within the group-as-a-whole rather than within each individual.

Summary

Systems thinking differs from more traditional thinking about groups in that it is systems-centered, not person-centered. The behavior of members in a group is therefore understood in terms of system dynamics rather than individual psychodynamics. The group-as-a-whole, its subgroups and its members are all defined as systems which mirror each other in dynamics, structure, and function. The most efficient method for facilitating the subgroup work of discrimination and integration is to encourage the exploration of experience within each individual subgroup before there is any cross-subgroup communication. Thus, by the very process of development, the internal process shifts from the cohesion around similarities to seeing differences in the cohesively similar. This process increases differentiation within each subgroup and increases the similarities between the subgroups. When boundaries become appropriately permeable to a transfer of information, similarities between the differing subgroups are perceived at the group-as-a-whole level, integration takes place and new subgroups can form. This is the process of system integration and transformation and the ongoing task of crossing from irreality to reality (and from the unconscious to the preconscious to the conscious). The very process of subgroups mirrors the dynamics of system development.

Systems-centered therapy is a method which capitalizes upon this principle in the group by deliberately promoting functional subgrouping to do the work of discriminating, communicating and integrating perceptions of differences in the apparently similar and similarities in the apparently different.

Series II: how to develop a working group

> inside the boundaries in space and time, group systems appear
> outside the boundaries in space and time, group systems disappear
> outside the group boundaries in space and time, social roles appear
> inside the group boundaries in space and time, member roles appear.

> boundaries define the difference
> between outside and inside
> between the past and the present and the future
> between the wishes and fears and the living reality
> between realities that change
> and realities that don't

> boundaries are the difference that makes the difference
> in managing the different demands
> of different times
> of different roles
> and of different places

> boundaries make it possible
> to stand at the fork-in-the-road
> to contain the energy in the system
> to explore the different paths
> to the primary and secondary goals

> boundaries make a group
> boundaries contain the work energy in the group and
> clear group goals serve as a light in the dark
> so that a group knows which direction to go

The purpose of developing a systems-centered group

When group reality is frustrating, the frustration generates tension, anxiety and rage. Containing frustration is necessary if the conflictual elements of group reality are to be identified and addressed rather than acted out or acted in.

The purpose of a systems-centered group is to keep both group and individual conflicts contained within the "system" of group-as-a-whole or subgroup structures, so that the group-as-a-whole can learn how to resolve conflicts, rather than relying on the individual members who will tend to respond to conflict in old, repetitive, defensive or stereotypic ways.

Subgrouping requires members to by-pass ambivalence and to join one side or another of the conflict. With opposing subgroups containing and exploring both sides of the issue, the group-as-a-whole and its members do not have to tie up energy defensively or discharge it into the environment. And when the group is ready to cross the boundaries between fantasies, wishes, fears, and actuality, it has the energy it needs to do its work.

Working groups are groups that work!

Systems-centered therapists teach groups to work as a system. As the system develops, so the group learns how to separate symptoms from problems, how to identify the particular defenses which prevent them from solving their problems, and how to work together to solve their problems.

Systems-centered therapy groups work together to develop a working group system with clear boundaries and goals. By developing a working system first, in which no person works alone, and every person has the support of their subgroup, working at therapy is not always so hard.

System boundaries

System boundaries define its existence in its environment. A system has boundaries in space and time. Space boundaries mark the threshold between the system inside and outside. Time boundaries differentiate between its past, present and the future. The state of the group boundaries determines the energy that is contained within the group for the work the group needs to do to reach its goals.

The context of boundaries

The environment around the group exists in space and time as a system of its own, and communications from the environment are always present at the boundary of the group system. At the beginning of each group, members cross from the environment outside the group to the environment inside the group. The events and climate of the environment will always have an influence at the beginning of each group. The distraught ward, the distracted clinic, or the disorganized office building will all influence the state of the member's system.

Monitoring system boundaries

Both the individual and the group have boundaries that separate them from other individuals and other groups in time and space. Both individual and group boundaries open and close to information—and whether they open or close depends upon how easily the information fits with how the system's store of information is currently organized. How each group and individual system develops is determined by how information crosses the boundary and how it is organized. (This is quite different from "what" is being said).

"Monitoring" group boundaries means that the systems-centered group leader will need to develop his perception of them—be able to "keep an eye" on what kinds of communication are happening where, and what those communications mean at all levels of the group. In other words, "to monitor the permeability of boundaries of all systems and sub-systems in the hierarchy".

This is important, because the energy available for group work is directly related to the condition of the group boundaries.

Boundaries in space and time

Make sure your group knows where and when to meet. The state of the group boundaries determines the energy that is contained within the group for the work the group needs to do to reach its goals.

Space boundaries: Where!

There is no group until it gets there—geographically and psychologically. It is important that all members know where the group is meeting and to be there—both physically and psychologically.

Space boundaries: Outside to inside

Here! Your first job is to get the energy contained within the group-as-a-whole system—crossing the boundaries from outside to inside. The clearer the group is about how to bring its outside experience into the group, rather than take flight into outside experience, the more relevant information and energy is available to reach the group goals.

Space boundaries: Inaccessible to accessible

How! Does personal information belong in the group or inside oneself? Another leader challenge! To reverse the personal tendency to withhold risky information that comes to mind in response to the group process, and to develop a norm in which the judgment as to whether information is useful data or not for group problem-solving belongs to the group, not the individual! The group cannot use information unless it is accessible.

It is helpful to draw group members' attention to an ignored fact of group life—that from the group perspective, no single member can take responsibility for how the group reacts to what a member says. If one stops and thinks, everyone has had the experience that one can say something one time and be completely ignored, and say the same thing another time and be heard! The message is the same but the group is different!

The other half of this way of orienting group members is to point out that every member has absolute responsibility for the effect on the group work of what they *withhold* from the group!

Time boundaries: When!

The group that is clear about its starting and stopping times can do their work in real world time and not be too distracted by fantasies that time is forever.

Crossing from the past and future into the present: Now!

Your leader job is to reverse a general tendency to cross the boundaries into the past or the future as a retreat from the problems in the present of the group.

The clearer the group becomes about using personal past and the present and the future as a source of information that is relevant to the work at hand, the more the group can put its past experience and future predictions to good use.

Role boundaries

Your job is to help group members not to take things personally! Everyone has had the experience of saying something only to see it disappear into the group without leaving a ripple, and then to see the same thing make a big splash a little while later! Bewildering, unless the member understands that the context determines the response, not the person. This is why it is important not to take things personally!

Taking roles personally is taking one's experience out of context. The personal *experience* of one's role is only part of the story: the part of the story that has to do with personal dynamics and history. The full story takes into account the social context: the group dynamics and the group history. Social forces have at least as much, and often more, to do with how members experience themselves in groups.

Every member does better if he can understand his group role impersonally and observe his behavior as it serves a function for the group-as-a-whole and how it relates to the goals. It is important to help your group learn early that the role one thinks one is playing and the way that the group is using the role are rarely the same. Group roles play a containing function for the group—and the hero or the villain leader, the scapegoat or the identified patient are all ways that a system "stores" information in a sub-system until the system-as-a-whole can integrate it. Thus the hero leader today is tomorrow's villain and today's scapegoat is tomorrow's pathfinder.

System goals

Keep the group goals in focus

Keep group goals in focus. Keep the group system related to the explicit environmental group goals in focus in the realities of space and time. Keep the group system related to the implicit survival and developmental goals in focus in the realities of system developmental issues and environmental influences. Keep the relationship between the explicit and implicit goals congruent.

Goals are primary and secondary, explicit and implicit

Keep reminding the group what its goal is. The group cannot work in the direction of its explicit goal if it doesn't keep it in mind. Goals orient the direction of the group energy. The group energy is always related to two kinds of goals:

Primary goals

Primary group goals are Internal System goals that relate to the survival and the development of the group.

When you help the group to maintain its boundaries (in space and time) you give the group healthy guidelines for both survival and development.

Secondary goals

Secondary goals are the External System goals that relate to the solving of the problems in mastering its environment.

Every system in the group, like the subgroups and members and the group-as-a-whole and you, has different problems to solve en route to their external goals.

Explicit goals

Explicit goals are goals that are explicit: the goals that are stated for the system, or the goals the system says it has! Explicit goals are not always the same as the implicit goal the goal—that is implied by the way the system behaves.

Implicit goals

Keep an eye on implicit goal behavior. If what the group is doing goes in the opposite direction to what the group is meant to be doing, the group will only have whatever energy it can spare from its implicit goal to do its work on its explicit goal.

When you see a group saying one thing and doing another, point it out to the group and ask what it will cost the group to move away from its explicit goal—and whether it is worth it. (Remember, it may be!)

Functional subgroups

Functional subgroups are subgroups that function so that no member needs to work alone. No member needs to take things personally. When one member gets stuck, another subgroup member takes the next step in problem-solving and when the stuck member is ready, he can join the subgroup work again. Every step a member takes is for himself, for his subgroup, and for the group-as-a-whole.

Keep the group-as-a-whole aware of its subgroups

Subgroups come together around similarities. Subgroup support encourages subgroup members to give information in a non-ambiguous, clear and audible voice, and to deepen the experience that they are subgrouping around.

Subgroups separate on differences

Subgroup dialogues exchange contradictory information across boundaries, process and integrate it. There is a big difference between stereotype subgroups and functional subgroups.

Keep individuals aware of their subgroup membership

Individuals can belong to more than one subgroup at the same time. This can be confusing and individuals may want to simplify their inner experience by being loyal to one at the expense of the other.

Encourage them to contain the conflict of belonging to more than one subgroup so that they can get the full benefit of their membership in each one.

Keep subgroups aware that their job is to join their members!

Orient people to the responsibility of publicly owning their subgroups. Acknowledging "joining" a subgroup is the first step to working in it.

Some advantages of functional subgrouping

Help subgroups become aware that the work of subgrouping is to build on what others of their subgroup members say, by sharing what is similar in their own resonating experience, and thus deepening the exploration of the issue that is at the heart of the subgroup. Avoid the emphasis of differences (which keeps people "safe and separate" from the impact of the resonance).

By encouraging subgrouping around the functional differences in the group instead of stereotyping them, differences are contained and explored first, before there is an attempt to resolve them superficially, or to fight over them instead. Subgroups contain for the group the conflicts in the group, by containing the splits while the group-as-a-whole develops methods of integrating them.

Summary: developing a working group

Systems-centered thinking solves a major problem for the therapist in that it is no longer necessary to think one way about individual dynamics and a different way about the dynamics of the group-as-a-whole. Individual and group system dynamics mirror each other— what therapists learn about one adds something new to what is known about the other. This is the second of the original four papers that accompany the Friends Hospital series on the systems-centered approach to group psychotherapy.

Subgrouping means that every step an individual member takes is for himself, for his subgroup, and for the group-as-a-whole.

Developing a Working Group means making clear boundaries to contain the work energy of the group and clear goals to direction it.

No member needs to work alone. No member needs to take things personally. When one member gets stuck, another subgroup member takes the next step in problem-solving and when the stuck member is ready, he can join the subgroup work again. Every step a member takes is for himself, for his subgroup, and for the group-as-a-whole.

Defense Modification means that from the first few minutes of the very first group, the systems-centered therapist influences group direction by teaching the group how to modify its defenses.

> *The journey is to*
> *drop the social defenses so that we can meet each other to begin with.*
> *differentiate between defenses, tension, anxiety and the emotional conflicts*
> *they mask.*
> *see how we build a group reality which no-one wants to live in.*
> *contain the frustration without acting out or acting in.*
> *accept the chaos of the unknown without blaming or labeling.*
> *and marvel at the emerging that we can't explain!*

Phases of Development require focusing the group on the defenses that exist in each specific phase. Defiance and compliance are directly related to the therapist in the first phase; suspiciousness, withdrawal, alienation and despair are related to intimacy with each other in the second, taking things "just" personally instead of existentially relates to the third phase.

Series III: defense modification: how to get through group defenses

> *Social Defenses:*
> *Airs and graces, the listening look*
> *the deflecting question*
> *and the ritual:*

"Good morning how are you? The weather
is fine! Did you hear about so and so?
Thanks for a wonderful time!"

Boundary Defenses:
Better the defeat in the past or future
than the unresolved fight in the present
Better the imaginary world of the paper tiger
than the unexplored jungle of now!

Role Lock Defenses:
Repeating one's role from before
is a skillful way of creating the reality
that one least wants to live in
but has survived once and can survive again!

Transforming Defenses:
Explaining instead of exploring
in lieu of transforming
separates the words of knowing in comprehension
from knowing without words in apprehension
and maintaining the status quo

Introduction

From the beginning of the group's life, the systems-centered therapist influences the direction of the group by teaching the group to
modify its defenses. There is a sequence to modifying defenses in a
group.

First the group drops the social defenses. Next the group learns
how to subgroup around work instead of around labeling, or rescu-
ing or blaming. Then the group learns the difference between the
defenses against frustration and the conflicts and mixed feelings
that are frustrating: that explaining and exploring lead in different
directions.

By exploring in subgroups, individuals learn to give up familiar explanations of why they do what they do. They discover that
the **experience** of their feelings is quite different from the way they
thought their feelings felt. In subgroups, they learn how to recognize

and undo defenses, and practice containing frustration instead of acting out or acting in.

As members explore their experience, the group-as-a-whole comes to understand that everyone's defenses characteristically build a group reality which no one wants to live in. By exploring instead of explaining, the group learns how to live in the present instead of the past and how to take old roles in new ways. It is in the world of existential reality that therapeutic change and all other kinds of transformation takes place.

The relationship between frustration and the defenses against the spontaneous self

Managing the conflicts of existential reality is frustrating.

Frustration

Frustration is full of energy, and is experienced as irritability. Irritability often arouses anxiety and tension.

Anxiety
Tension
Irritability

When frustration is contained, the frustrating experience can be addressed, and there is plenty of energy for managing the conflict. When frustration is not contained, anxiety, tension and irritability become the problem.

The defenses against anxiety, tension and irritability are cognitive, psychosomatic and behavioral.

Cognitive Defenses
Psychosomatic Defenses
Behavioral Defenses

Cognitive, psychosomatic and behavioral defenses bind, constrict, or discharge the energy that was originally available for working out conflicts.

Defenses Create Secondary Symptoms
Secondary Symptoms Pre-empt the Primary Problem

Defenses not only bind, constrict, or discharge the energy, but become symptoms that pre-empt the original problem.

Cognitive defenses

Cognitive defenses construct a secondary reality based on fear. The "solution" of a secondary reality generates still more anxiety, tension and irritability, as well as other secondary experiences like guilt and dread and worrying. By fleeing to defensively constructed reality, a person still has all the problems that existed in the primary reality and all the problems generated by the secondary reality as well.

Psychosomatic defenses

Psychosomatic defenses involve us with physical symptoms and muscular aches and pains instead of the original conflict.

Tension induced muscular aches and pains, and the symptoms of anxiety or irritability are uncomfortable, but not dangerous. These can be worked with in the group just like any other defenses. Non-benign conversion symptoms however, can be dangerous.

Conversion symptoms need to be "reconverted" before any other defense modification is done. No work that increases frustration, and therefore increases anxiety, tension and irritability and the psychosomatic defenses against them, should be done until the tendency to channel defenses into the body has been de-conditioned.

Behavioral defenses

Acting out an internal conflict instead of understanding it makes for double trouble: trouble is transferred to the outside world leaving the inner conflict still further away from any kind of acceptance or solution. Bringing old solutions to new situations makes new situations into old.

Cognitive, Psychosomatic and Behavioral Defenses Bind, Constrict and Discharge Energy

We can learn how to contain the energy in frustration, together with the anxiety, tension and irritability that goes with it, while we experience the mixed feelings we have about the conflicts that arise in our relationship to ourselves, to others and to the outside world. This is how we learn to "create" all the worlds we live in!

We can learn not to "emigrate" to a secondary, defensively constructed world that makes things worse instead of better.

We can learn how to "return" to our primary world by "undoing" our defenses, making contact with our primary conflict and restore our primary selves.

Sequence of defense modification in systems-centered psychotherapy groups

When we explain to ourselves and to others why we do what we do, we are using a map of the world and ourselves that we already know. Taking the journey to the inner self means exploring the parts of ourselves we don't know. Our guide is our experience, and we make the map of the journey as we go. To do this, every time we come to a fork-in-the-road we need to choose the road to exploring and not the road to explaining.

First stage—defending and explaining

Lower the Group Anxiety by exploring the cognitive explanations. Exploring and explaining move in opposite directions!

Move Through the Cognitive Defenses by checking the secondary reality against the primary reality and adjusting it to fit. Exploring reality changes the kind of explaining!

Move Through Tension like dissolving a straight jacket and free the inner feeling from constraint. Exploring instead of explaining moves in the direction of feeling!

Accept that frustration has anxiety, tension and irritability as constant companions

Defenses are work! Defenses use up energy.

Containing and Exploring

Explore the Conflict! Explore for the conflict between the self and one's internal or external world that is generating frustration.

Recognize Mixed Feelings! Hate and love; pain and pleasure; disappointment and hope; compliance and defiance; passivity and activity.

Recognize the Repeating Roles: Victim, bully, scapegoat, identified patient.

Move Through the Barriers: Exploring the experience means moving through the barriers: stubbornness, passivity, withdrawal.

Barrier experiences like stubbornness, shame, humiliation, shyness and embarrassment, are the thresholds between the defended self and the primary self.

By banishing spontaneity with oneself and with others, the shamed self can survive forever without feeling ashamed behind the barriers erected of the stubborn self.

Learning how to cross through the barrier experiences without turning back is the way to liberating the lost and imprisoned part of the inner self.

Humiliation and shame hide the spontaneous, responsive, primary self (that was originally shamed) from the defended self.

Shyness and embarrassment hide the spontaneous, responsive primary self from others.

Recognize Primary Experience: The spontaneous—responsive—existential self.

Locating Defenses Across the Boundaries Between Constructed Reality and Experienced Reality in the Past, Present and Future

Series IV: subgrouping in the phases of group development

First Phase: Authority

Two subgroups balance the power and control
a flight into pleasing compliance
a fight in rebellious defiance
fear of a murderous rage
and the wish for a magical cure.

Second Phase: Intimacy

Two subgroups balance closeness
too far for some—too close for others

enchantment and disappointment
suspicion, alienation, despair,
and the emptiness of being together alone!

Third Phase: Goal and Context

Through frustration and the prison of stubbornness
through enchantment and despair's black hole
Through apprehension to apprehension
to the transformational goal
in the context of the group-as-a-whole.

Sometimes the context for change is the self
sometimes the subgroup or group-as-a-whole
the systems-centered member
relates each task to the context and goal.

Introduction

The phases of development of a systems-centered group are the context in which individual developmental issues are revisited and re-mastered.

Applying a systems-centered approach to psychotherapy makes it possible to use a common language to describe the stages of development of all the human "systems" that concern the group therapist: the member, the subgroup and the group-as-a-whole.

Systems do not exist in the real world like people do. Systems exist only in the mind.

Systems come into existence when you think them, and disappear when you don't. Thinking "systems" is only useful if systems thinking permits you to do things in reality that you could not do before you thought in terms of systems.

Putting systems-centered theory into practice has made it possible not only to talk about individual and group behavior from a common perspective, but to influence both the potential and the course of individual and group-as-a-whole development.

The group therapist is able to influence **system dynamics** in the direction of developmental goals, confident that effecting change in any one system will influence all. In other words, influencing development in a member or a subgroup or in the group-as-a-whole will influence the developmental potential of the system hierarchy.

Differences in the systems-centered approach to group therapy

Human systems are made, not born. In the systems-centered approach to the phases of development in group psychotherapy, the group is not left to develop "naturally" while the therapist "contains" the process and judiciously interprets it to make it conscious to the group, as is the case when the approach is primarily psychodynamic. Rather, group forces are deliberately exploited; certain group behaviors deliberately encouraged and others discouraged; all dynamics, however primitive, are legitimized so that they can be explored and understood. For example, predictable occurrences, like the creation of identified patients and scapegoating, are no longer predetermined in a systems-centered group. When subgroups, rather than individuals, contain different sides of predictable group "splits" and when the group-as-a-whole is required to "contain" the conflict consciously as a working task, it is no longer necessary to delegate difference to a scapegoat, an identified patient or a deviant pair. Deliberately splitting basic group conflicts into two containing subgroups, which come together around similarities, and within which members recognize their differences, leads to differentiation within the system at all levels of the hierarchy.

The technique of functional subgrouping

From the systems perspective, it may be too much for individual members to contain both their own and the group conflicts in development. In the systems approach, the individual is not required to "contain" conflict, but rather to use the mechanism of "splitting" functionally by deliberately "projecting" one side of the conflict into a working subgroup. Both sides of the conflict are explored separately in different subgroups. In this way, the technique of functional subgrouping enables conflicts to be contained in the system of the group-as-a-whole. As the two subgroups differentiate, so it becomes possible for subgroup members to recognize differences within their subgroup and differences between the subgroups. When differences are perceived in a context that makes them not "too different", it becomes possible for integration to occur within the group-as-a-whole. New integration in turn introduces a potential for integration within the individual members that did not exist before the subgroup work was done. Differences, initially too conflictual for individual systems to contain, when projected into subgroups, can be re-introjected and integrated after the process of discrimination and integration has occurred through subgroup containment. It is in this way that splits are deliberately "projected" into, and "contained" by, the group-as-a-whole.

In systems-centered groups, the primary task is to develop an interdependent problem-solving system so that the work of therapy is done in the process of learning how to do the work of therapy. From the first few minutes of the very first group, members are encouraged to work interpersonally, to talk to the group or to a particular member, and to stay connected, rather than to withdraw into themselves with their pain. This sets up a work style of supportive mirroring, which is key to the power of functional subgrouping. Members learn to work in subgroups by recognizing the difference between saying "I'm in your subgroup" (which is rather like waving) and joining and working (which is like getting into the boat and rowing!).

There also is an emphasis on developing a climate in which reality can be tested and problems can be solved. The first step for group members is to distinguish between the primary and secondary reality: the group members will learn how to tell the difference between the feelings that are induced by the way we explain the world and the feelings that are primary responses to the way we experience the world. For example, members in systems-centered groups learn to recognize that explaining is almost always accompanied by upward eye movements and a sensation in the head, whereas eyes tend to turn downward and inward while exploring, with sensations in the abdomen (frequently rage) or the chest (frequently grief).

Group reality is frustrating. People have a tendency to try to "explain away" conflicts in the here-and-now. Defensive explanations, however, tend to create an alternate reality, a second world which reflects the anxiety, tension and irritation that conflicts arouse, and tend to make things worse rather than better. This secondary world then generates secondary problems. The distress born of catastrophic thoughts is no less distressing for being manufactured. Many of the problems that people bring to group therapy are secondary problems generated by their defenses against the conflicts which exist in their primary reality.

Thus, in a systems-centered group, recognizing and naming feelings and explaining the meaning of their free-associations is not the whole story. Members are also encouraged to allow themselves to fill up with the **experience** of the feelings as they have them, and to see whether or not the explanation of the experience is in reality the experience that they "think" or "say" it is. Often, of course it is not! For example, members are almost always surprised to find that the experience of anger is often, in fact, exciting, freeing and empowering, and it is the way they think about it that make it unpleasant. This often means that members of the group learn for the first time that shouting or swearing or throwing a tantrum is not the *experience* of rage, but rather, the *expression* of it. This often also means that members recognize how much of their emotion is generated by their defenses against their primary experience rather than by the primary experience itself.

Technically, the work of the systems-centered group is to understand that conflict occurs at every boundary crossing. In crossing a boundary, something changes, and changes always require some resolution of conflict. All conflict is frustrating, and all frustration mobilizes energy. Frustration often generates anxiety, tension and irritability. Anxiety, tension and irritability are not problems in themselves. It is the defenses against them that make for problems.

A major focus for systems-centered group members is to learn to tell the difference between the symptoms that result from binding or discharging the frustration aroused by conflict, and the conflict itself that is pulling them in opposite directions. They learn that feelings have no intrinsic value other than as important signals of the state of well-being of their system. They learn about the human tendency to take refuge from conflicts in internal and external reality by explaining their experience in ways that take them away from the here-and-now; that these explanations construct a secondary reality which then generates a secondary set of feelings. Work in a systems-centered group is different from the work of free-associating until comprehension and insight occurs. Rather, it is learning how to focus attention and follow the feelings, like a signal, systematically moving through the defenses, until there is non-verbal apprehension, a condensation of experience. Finding the words to describe what the person knows without words in this flash of insight may take many hours, and even weeks—sometimes the rest of the life. The goal of systems-centered therapy is for members to learn how to arrive at both comprehension and apprehension: the twins of insight.

The phases of development of a systems-centered group are the context in which individual developmental issues are revisited and re-mastered. Group members mature as the group learns to work and to love and to play! (Agazarian, 1992).

There is little doubt that a predictable sequence of developmental dynamics is there to be seen if the therapist knows what to look for. When observed, the different phases of group development can be seen to have a significant effect on the dynamics of the group-as-a-whole and of the individuals in groups. There are many paths to a goal. The goals in systems-centered therapy are the same as the goals of psychodynamic therapy, but the ways of reaching them are different. The development of a group results from an inter-play of the same forces that characterize the process of development of any human system: separation, individuation, integration and transformation. All human systems move from primal dependence to independence, and the course is determined by successive integrations of approach and avoidance forces. From the systems-centered perspective, these forces are understood to be the same as those described by Bennis and Shepard (1956) in the Theory of Group Development, but they are addressed differently. For example, they are not interpreted as a property of "dependent" compliant or "counter dependent" defiant *individuals* but rather as approach and avoidance forces that are contained in subsystems of systems—and exist simultaneously at the system levels of the individual member, subgroup and the group-as-a-whole. Similarly, the development of group interdependence is determined by successive integrations by subgroups that contain the dynamics of approach, expressed in blind trust and fusion on the one hand, and avoidance, expressed in blind mistrust and alienation on the other. Again, it is the integration of the forces contained in these two subgroups that determines the development of system separation and individuation which is a dynamic that operates concurrently in both the group and the individual member throughout the phases of development of the group-as-a-whole.

Discussed in greater detail in the sections below are both the predictable sequence of events that characterize each phase and subphase of the development of groups. Also discussed is the influence on the manifestations of those dynamics that are introduced by applying the systems-centered framework. The description of the group behavior is in both cases taken from my own direct experience working with therapy groups and training groups as they struggle with the different issues along the road to their maturity.

Overview of phase one: leader oriented (authority)

The surface issues addressed at the beginning of every group are issues of power and control. Preoccupation with authority and the pecking order make for a competitive and political climate, in which information is currency. Member relates to member with one eye on therapist in a series of apparently dyadic interactions that are functionally triadic.

There are two predictable subphases in Phase One, the first a more passive phase of flight, and a second more active fight phase during which the group progresses from passive stereotyping to active scapegoating, first of each other and then of the therapist. In the passive phase, the group "identified patient" role is created to contain the group's passive and helpless dependency, offered to the "good" therapist to nurture and cherish. In the active phase, the group "scapegoat" role is created to contain the active deviance, in an attempt to bind the murderous rage so that the bad therapist is not destroyed.

Undirected, these phases predictably move from flight into passive compliance and sorties into active defiance. There is spasmodic scapegoating and in-fighting until the group aggression is focused on the therapist. Scapegoating the therapist is not always overtly hostile. It can be manifested by covertly seducing the therapist into membership or denigrating the therapist as an incompetent. In fact, in therapy groups as distinct from training groups, it is sometimes easier for the group to overthrow authority covertly rather than with an overt challenge of active rebellion. When the group successfully challenges and overthrows authority, the group temporarily resolves its conflict about good and evil by splitting, locating "evil" in the "bad" therapist, and "good" in the group. This is called the "Barometric Event" in that after a successful confrontation of the therapist, the group energy is freed from the compelling struggle with the therapist over power and control and is turned, instead, into issues of intimacy. Below are the descriptions of the subphases in the group journey through the phase of Authority.

Subphase I: flight

Subphase I is characterized by group behavior that is predominantly dependent, stereotypic and conforming. Subgroups form around similarities that are mainly irrelevant to the goals of the group but are highly relevant to political survival.

The passively compliant part of the self tends to be obedient, conforming, pleasing, adaptive, and lovingly merging with blind trust: given to flight and avoidance and "love". Members, with most salience for this response, subgroup spontaneously and easily around their similarities. It is often a member of the passive compliant subgroup who is volunteered by the group to be the identified patient in the early stages of the group.

This early phase in a systems-centered group is where the major work is done with the defenses. It is in this phase that the group learns to tell the difference between the feelings that arise from the inner conflicts, and the symptoms that result from the defenses against the anxiety, tension and irritability that is engendered by the frustration that these inner conflicts arouse.

Analysis of the containing role of identified patient, explored in subgroups around the "helper" and the "helpee", enable insight into the characteristic constellation of defenses that set up the passive, helpless victim in all its different manifestations. It is through this work that the first work with "projective identification" is done through exploring the human tendency to split off and project the "hurt" part of the self into another, and then try to "cure" it. In the systems approach to group therapy, the group learns to make use of the natural tendency to split the good from the bad and to **consciously** contain the split in separate subgroups. In order for subgrouping to do the work of containing and integrating the group split, every member of the group must "pick a side" so that no part of the group remains uncommitted or ambivalent.

Transitional stage from flight and compliance to fight and defiance

The transition from flight to fight is the transition from passive to active. An actively compliant subgroup may try to bully other members into compliance with authority; and a defiant subgroup may emerge in overt or covert defiance to authority. The transition into the fight phase marks also a transition from the social defenses and defenses against anxiety into the character defenses, particularly stubbornness. Stubbornness is characteristically used whenever autonomy is threatened. The tragedy of stubbornness is that it saves the inner life but makes it impossible to experience or live it.

Characteristic defenses unwittingly replicate, in the present of the group, the role-relationships learned in the past. The work of identifying the function of the containing role of victim for the group in the first subphase leads to a better understanding of the function of the scapegoat role in the second subphase.

Subphase of fight

The fight subphase is characterized by group behavior that is predominantly contentious—political pairing for control.

Defiant subgroups tend to be rebellious, non-conforming, resistant to influence, stubborn, individualistic, contentious and authoritarian, given to initiating a stand against group issues, and ultimately to leading the group in a rebellion against the therapist.

Group relationships shift constantly as the tides change in the group. Scapegoating a member functions as a "merging" for group, an integration of the subgroup in relation to a common enemy, therefore the scapegoat is an integrative agent for the group (just as the identified patient was an integrative solution in the flight subphase) and it also serves as a trial run. The group, discovering that it can survive scapegoating, and coming together as a group-as-a-whole around the resolution of scapegoating, does the necessary membership work to enable it to take on the therapist.

The systems-centered approach offers an alternative to scapegoating and in-fighting in the fight phase of group development. In the first subphase, systems-centered members are introduced to the idea that they project into others that which they are not able to address in themselves. However, repossessing the projections instead of acting out on a scapegoat is a more difficult task than repossessing the hurt self from the identified patient. In the case of scapegoating, it is the unacceptable parts of the self that are projected into the scapegoat and treated as unacceptable. This leads to deepening the learning about the process of attempting to "take back" whatever parts of themselves they can identify: either through recognizing a disowned similarity, or by recognizing a suspicious absence of any similarities. Again, group members are encouraged to choose the subgroup to join that would be most useful to each one of them in their work. Ambivalence is treated as a defense against experiencing the conflict, and subgrouping as a way of working with one side of the conflict, whether or not the individual is aware of both sides. In this way, whether the issue is to split and deny one half of the split, or to split and contain both halves, each individual member works with only one, in the context of subgroup support, until the natural development of subgrouping raises the other side in the group.

Transition from leader oriented (Phase I)
to group oriented (Phase II)

The "Barometric Event" is the fulcrum that catapults the group from Phase One into Phase Two. A crisis around the love-hate split ... and the crisis where there's only room for one.

Throughout this phase, and indeed, throughout the life of the group, the therapist's responsibility is to contain the group projective identifications until the group-as-a-whole can contain those dynamics itself. The therapist role serves as a container for the group-as-a-whole good/bad split: while the group crosses the boundary between fantasy and reality—the fantasy of the good/idealized and bad/devalued therapist into the reality of the de-idealized function of the therapist.

It is certainly obvious that Phase One has to do with social issues of power and control. However, the preoccupation with the politics of power and control are the result of defensive maneuvers that protect the system from frustrations that are inherent in dependency, and the deeper annihilation anxiety that is aroused in the separation/individuation struggle. The therapeutic goal of Phase One development therefore is to restore functional dependency. Nothing human can be achieved unless a functional dependency can be developed among the members, in relationship to the therapist, for the life and work of the group.

In the first phase of group, the underlying fears of dependency are expressed in terms of annihilation: kill or be killed, with resultant guilt and blame. Murderous rage "turned in" relates to the "over dependent", depressive, guilty, compliant, passive response to dependency disappointment. Rage "turned out" relates to the "counter dependent", counter-phobic, blameful, rebellious, active response to dependency disappointment. In the heat of the baro-metric event, these fears are expressed openly. Members, in different groups, will express the same sentiments, in a varying range and intensity of grief, guilt and fear. "There is only room for one of us!" "It's either you or me!" This will be familiar to individual therapists in the heat of the negative (essentially paranoid) transference where the belief is that only the patient or the therapist can survive and there cannot be room for both.

It is with great relief that the group accesses primitive, and often very bloody and violent fantasies, of the destruction of the thera-pist. Sometimes the therapist is seen as some animal, murdered and thrown into the middle of the group, and savaged. Sometimes the members experience themselves as violent and bloody animals feed-ing on the carcass, with blood dripping from their face. Other times the therapist is thrown onto a fire, a pyre, danced around, roasted and eaten. Sometimes a duality is experienced: the impulse to rend and tear at flesh in savage hunger, and at the same time, to swal-low and digest and be satisfied and full inside. Often, the work is followed by a rush of gratitude and love that the therapist can con-tain so much hate. And afterwards, in the relief, there can be a pro-found feeling of group communion.

In groups that access less primal levels, seduction or devaluation methods are used to undermine the authority of the therapist. There can be a symbolic communion around the therapist as an alterna-tive to the underlying savagery. Once a group passed one small pep-permint patty around which the group managed so that each of its fourteen members broke off a piece. Devaluation can defeat author-ity by rendering it bumbling and incompetent. One group became convinced that I was aging beyond reason, and held no future for them. Another decided that I did not know enough about groups to help, and seriously considered the task of trying to train me, and yet another wanted to keep me around affectionately as a pet.

Whereas the basic work of recognizing and struggling with defen-ses is done in the earlier stages of the group, it is the authority issue that puts the work to the test. The early work on containment ena-bles the group to regress within its group-generated structure. It is within the safety of this group "surrogate ego" that the regression in the service of therapy is done, with little risk that the group will actually act out the sadism. Typically, of course, the more available and primitive and bloody and savage the primary images, the easier it is for the group to move past the sadistic fantasies, the more relief the group experiences, and the more wholeheartedly they move on to the next phase. This is compatible, of course, with the understanding that the deeper the unconscious access, the less the denial and repression and reaction formations and paranoid ideation will distort the inner experience and the greater the potential for transformation.

The most difficult experience of the barometric event, more likely in a group-as-a-whole approach that does not include systems training, is when the sadism that underlies the murderous rage breaks through the containment in the group-as-a-whole and expresses itself as a group level paranoid delusion, generating a "real" experience of the therapist as toxic and destructive, with concomitant threats, either of real murder or symbolic character assassination. This can also take the form of the group unconsciously electing a member with salience for the role to express sadistic virulence for the group without the group being able to subgroup functionally. In both cases, the steady insistence of subgrouping around the issues, and a consistent emphasis on the containment of boundaries and a focus on goals will typically, sooner or later, contain the dynamics so that they can be integrated.

Overview of phase two: group oriented

Intimacy engenders more complex dynamics than issues with authority in that the dynamics are more primal and therefore the defenses against the primary dynamics are more complex. The major split is into "passive merging" and "actively alienated" subgroups organized around overpersonal, counterpersonal and interpersonal forces. In this second phase, subgroups balance closeness: too far for some, too close for others. Enchantment and disappointment, suspicion, alienation, despair and the emptiness of being together alone!

The experience of paranoid suspiciousness in the second phase of development is not the rationalized paranoid world of the first phase which is no more or no less difficult to endure than the French revolution. The suspicious, paranoid world of the second phase is the objectless world of Kafka—where the location of threat is nowhere and everywhere. It is the world familiar to every adult who remembers what every child forgets: where intuitions of reality make no external sense; where interpretations from reality make no internal sense; and nowhere is the language for making sense spoken.

In the transition between the therapist-centered first phase and the group-centered second phase, the disappointing therapist is rejected as an object and the good group takes his place. Whereas in the first subphase of Phase One, all is right with the world as long as the good therapist exists, in the first subphase of Phase Two, all is right with the world as long as the good group exists.

Just as in the "dependency" first phase, the outcome of the struggle with authority is influenced by the balance in the conformist (dependent) and rebellious (counter dependent) subgroups who contain for the group the split between defiance and compliance; so, in the second "interdependent" phase, the outcome of the issues in intimacy is influenced by the balance between counterpersonal and overpersonal subgroups that contain for the group the split between blind trust and blind mistrust.

In systems-centered group development, encouraging the group to split into two containing subgroups, one containing the salience for closeness and the other containing the salience for distance, permits both sides of the experience to be explored simultaneously, and makes it unnecessary to work through the second phase in two separated phases of enchantment and disenchantment. Thus blind trust can be explored in relationship to blind mistrust; the wish for merging and fusion and togetherness can be explored in relationship to the fear of engulfment, the retreat into isolation and alienation. As the exploration of the experiences deepens and differentiates, the different issues can be recognized, contained, integrated and reintegrated through the many levels of work that are required in this phase.

Group oriented—subphase I: enchantment

In the symbiotic ambience of this phase, members experience a euphoric relief. It is as if the dreams of mirroring have become a reality, and that the group is truly a holding environment.

The enchanted, merging subgroup contains the blind trust of the group and each other. For the enchanted subgroup, relationships can never be too close.

Differences, when they intrude into the enchantment of similarity, can be experienced with all the pain of a break in mirroring. In disappointment, the group is "dropped" into the pain of disenchantment and suspicion, precipitating the group into the next phase, full of despairing mistrust of each other, the group and the self.

Transitional stage: from enchantment (group oriented phase I) to disenchantment (group oriented phase II)

For the enchanted subgroup, containing the blind trust in the group, relationships can never be too close. However, for some, relationships are always threatening when they become too close. And in a developing group, blind mistrust does not remain split off and denied forever. In the transitional stage, one moment all seems right with the world, at the next moment it all looks too good to be true. The tension between the forces of blind trust and blind mistrust results in the emergence of wariness in what was an enchanted group. A suspicious subgroup gives voice to the concern that all is not quite what it seems and disenchantment enters the group.

There is a relationship between the ability to develop some functional dependency upon the therapist and how virulent the paranoid threshold will be as the group moves into disenchantment. Suspiciousness and the "paranoia" protect against shame and humiliation by projection. When this defense does not hold, there is the experience of unbearable shame and humiliation, which is retreated from in a painful withdrawal. The group-as-a-whole is no longer full of warm interpersonal affective responses. Instead a pervasive disenchantment results in a grim, "responsible" joyless knowledge that survival is at the price of being forever alone.

Group oriented—subphase II: disenchantment

First comes the suspiciousness which makes for distance and reduces intimacy, thus requiring the system to shift from the phase of enchantment to the phase of disenchantment. There is great disappointment in the transition work when the group is working hard to deny the conflicted feelings in relationship to the group and each other.

The suspicious subgroup contains the wariness of the group—the concern that all is not quite what it seems. One moment all seems right with the world, at the next moment it all looks too good to be true.

Potentially, the group can take advantage of the emerging feelings of disappointment by learning to own some of the more difficult of the interpersonal feelings, like jealousy or envy, which, when defended against, make for alienation and distance. When this work is kept in focus, as it is in systems groups, then the transition into alienation and despair does not become an overwhelming and alienating experience and can be explored and contained by functional subgrouping.

Suspiciousness disrupts the climate of the group and at the same time increases the need to develop reality-testing mechanisms, thus shifting from the phase of disenchantment to the phase of consensual validation. Suspiciousness "denied" leaves the system doomed to the homoeostatic mechanism of blind trust and fixated in the phase of disenchantment. In systems-centered group work, mechanisms of reality-testing have been developed from the inception of the group. Thus, if the salience for suspicion is not too great in the group, this work is done with relatively little difficulty.

The disenchanted, alienated subgroup contains the blind mistrust of the group and each other. For the disenchanted subgroup, relationships are always threatening when they become too close.

Within the schizoid withdrawal there are the associations to the black hole, being in outer space without a life line, cold, in the Ice Age, empty, hollow, forever in despair, hopeless. When this defense is threatened there is a desperate "holding on" so that one does not "disintegrate, fall apart". When the group is encouraged to regress into and through the "feared disintegrative" experience, the group reaches an understanding at the group level that there is a "shared" alienation, and therefore an existential common experience.

The individual work at this time is the work of "letting go" and "falling into" the black hole, finding the way by following the affective signal of dread. A further retracing step, past the despair, is the original betrayal of the true self by whatever shaming experience created a split between the spontaneous self and the self that was shamed (probably in the process of being socialized). Thus paranoia and despair are the last ditch defenses against the anguish of shame. The consequences of the defenses are the permanent absence of that part of the self in intimate relationships, either with the true self or with any significant other, which results in the schizoid feelings of emptiness. (In truth, the self has been "emptied out", and the inconsolable grief is at its absence.)

This work, of course, is greatly facilitated by the resonance of a subgroup. As was illustrated in the episode around the barometric event, one member's work takes the subgroup forward, and when that individual member can go no further, another member picks up and carries on. When one or two members have survived the fear of disintegration and loss of the self, and discover the spontaneous experience behind the original shaming, the map is made from group experience and other members can follow. It is in this phase that members learn that they continue to shame the spontaneous experience that was split off in the original shaming. They learn that they are now shaming themselves as they were once shamed. In one group, for example, where the group was working with inhibitions around sex, two members were building on each other's childhood experience: one caught showing his penis to another boy, and one caught masturbating. It seemed that it was only the first member who was able to move past the memories of his terrible punishment to the original pleasure and pride in himself and in his younger friend's admiration. When, however, he shyly shared his sudden full experience of physical sexuality with the group, the other member was able to join the work, and own that she too had a full sexual experience and was hiding it behind her shyness.

Transition across the barrier affects

This is an important sequence for the group to map. The journey through the barrier affects, like shame, into a triumphant recovery of the original feelings that were a spontaneous part of themselves before they were shamed, a brief struggle to free themselves from the impulse to keep the new-found selves hidden, to a final journey through a new shyness as they shared the secret feelings with the group—again in contact with some significant other and again working for their subgroup. Again it is the fear of the defenses that bind or discharge the energy of the feeling that increase the intensity of the journey. For example, one member regaining his full sexual experience became embarrassed that he would actually not be able to contain it and would have an orgasm. Reminding him that it was his choice to choose how and where he wanted to "discharge" his sexual energy freed him to share his joy with the group.

It is no coincidence that annihilation anxiety is aroused when these defenses are threatened. The group is in a conflict between the courage to explore and the terror of the inner experience to be explored, which requires facing the fear of personal disintegration. There is typically a last ditch, defensive stand, a schizoid withdrawal into outer space—an implosion into the black hole, a turning of the face away from any re-experience of the original annihilation shame. Each defense is, of course, perfectly syntonic with the experience against which it is defending. In a real sense, that part of the self that was shamed was annihilated, and did, for all intents and purposes, die (and is grieved). The group truth, of course, is that there are many other selves alive and well but in hiding. Group development calls on many different aspects of the self to re-emerge and take part in the developing group.

Working on the difficult task of traversing the barriers of shame and humiliation into the core self, first one and then another group member hesitantly expressed a wish to be the center of the group's attention and also expressed concern that if any one member got all the attention there would be none left for anyone else. During the subgroup work of separating out "wanting" and "getting", the exhilarating freedom of being *able* to want broke through. "I want to be the center!" "Me too!" "I want to be grandiose!" "I want to be narcissistic" "I want it all!" In the delighted pause that followed the euphoria, the group noticed that there had been plenty of room for everyone. "The more we want to be, the more room there is!"

Transitional stage from phase two (group orientation)
to phase three (context orientation)

From the understanding that the "whole group" has the potential for an alienated and alone experience comes the gradual testing of reality—the ability to call a spade a spade. In the transition from a developing group to a mature group, the group uses subgrouping as the major developmental force, containing the maturational process of splitting in the group-as-a-whole while the splits are integrated through membership in discriminating subgroups. Integration leads to transformation into an awareness of context as the primary determiners of individual and group experience.

Phase three: goal and context oriented

In Phase Three there is containment; the inner balancing of the love, the hate and the many transformations of reality. It is almost as if, once the group has experienced being able to survive as a group, the descent into the primary experience of abandonment of self and other in the black hole of despair, the transformation occurs, transmuting the original fear that to grow separate is to die to understanding that it is the way to survive and live in ever increasing complexity in the hierarchy of human systems.

The work of the mature group is to enable transactions across the boundaries. In the ongoing group life of work, the issues themselves do not change, but the ability to work with them does.

Series V: building blocks of a theory of living human systems and its systems-centered practice

> *Systems-centered groups work with clear boundaries and goals.*
> *Sometimes the context for change is the self,*
> *sometimes the subgroup or the group-as-a-whole.*
> *The context of work through which systems transform*
> *fits the role to the task and the task to the context and goal.*

There are three "living human systems" that can be seen when one looks at a therapy group through systems-centered eyes: the member system, the subgroup system, and the system of the group-as-a-whole. Each of these different systems is similar in that their structure and function can be described using the same words. They are different in that each is at a different level in the hierarchy of living human systems, and therefore as one shifts from one level to another, the context of experience changes, and so do the roles that the systems play and so do the goals of those roles.

This article defines and discusses the four terms that are basic to understanding a theory of living human systems and to doing systems-centered therapy. These are: isomorphy, hierarchy, structure and function.

Isomorphy

Isomorphy is the word used in General Systems Theory (von Bertalanffy, 1969; Durkin, 1981) to say that every system in a defined hierarchy is similar in structure and function. This is probably the single most important thought to keep in mind for all systems-centered leaders in that it allows you to understand that however different an individual member may look from a subgroup or the group-as-a-whole, each in fact has certain common factors which can be recognized in their structure and in their function. A systems-centered orientation applies to any level of system intervention, whether it be a member, a subgroup or the group-as-a-whole. A systems-centered orientation also recognizes that systems do not exist in a vacuum. Systems exist in a hierarchy in which every system exists in the environment above it and is the environment for the system below it.

Hierarchy

Thinking in the context of hierarchy is important for systems-centered therapists because every system exists in the environment of the system above it, and is the environment of the system below it. When therapists think hierarchically, their understanding shifts according to the level of hierarchy they are thinking about. In other words, as the context changes, so do the requirements and implications for change. Interventions intended to facilitate the work within the self-system are different from the interventions that are intended to influence the subgroup work, and different again when they are intended to facilitate the transition between the self-system and the systems-centered role. It is, of course, extremely important to keep in mind the impact of change at any one level of a system on other levels of the organization. A useful change at one level is not always useful if it interferes with the efficiency at another level. For example, at the beginning of a systems-centered group all interventions are targeting towards the self-system, so that members can bring their energy into the group and focus it on the group goals. However, as soon as members are present and focused, the target of interventions is towards connecting the members to subgroups, so that differences can be recognized and integrated through functional subgrouping rather than acted out in stereotypical or repetitive ways.

Thinking about any one living human systems means thinking about the whole hierarchy of systems as well as each system that makes it up. There is a hierarchical relationship between a team, a department or an organization and also for a member of a team, a department or an organization. Systems are ideas that exist only in the mind—they do not exist in the real world like people do. Thinking about systems is useful when it helps one to intervene in a group in ways that one might not be able to if one's thinking was confined to the people in it.

When one thinks about a "member" system (remembering that the word "system", like the word "member", stands for an idea and not a person), one thinks about a person as a "member of their self-system" in a different way from when one thinks about them as a member of a subgroup or as a member of the group-as-a-whole. At each level of the hierarchy, the member has a different role, different goals, and different relationships to the other systems of the hierarchy.

Context defines what is relevant to think about when one thinks about member as a living human system rather than the living person that is occupying the role. How you think about a person depends less on him or her personally and more on the context that you are thinking about him or her in. As the context changes, so do the roles and the goals.

Taking things just personally

The major difference between taking things personally and not taking things personally is the ability to see things in context. When you take things personally, you become the center of whatever happens around yourself—all the good things in the environment make you feel good and all the bad things in the environment make you feel bad. Taking things personally is rather like being the center of your own world—you are a system all to yourself—and your self-system is the only context. In this sense, taking things personally is taking things out of context! In systems-centered thinking it is as if the system no longer existed in an environment. When one takes things in context, every single thing has many different meanings depending upon the context from which you are experiencing it.

A good example of this is the system that constructs a reality without being able to test it in reality. In other words, all communications are trapped inside the self-system without the necessary transactions across the reality-irreality boundary. Unless the irreality-reality boundary is crossed, it serves as an impermeable barrier and defines the context of experience. As long as a person is living in the constructed reality of their thoughts, they are existing "as if" there was no other reality. This is the systems-centered barrier experience, and in every barrier experience, however generated, the only context that exists for the person is the self.

There is always a conflict at every boundary. You cannot cross a boundary without turning your attention away from one side of the boundary and towards the other. However many times you make the journey, no matter how well you know the way, you always have to fight against the impulse to take short cuts. Crossing a boundary is frustrating.

It takes work, a conscious shift of attention, to turn away from one direction and pay attention to another. Your whole system changes its context every time you cross a boundary. It makes different discriminations and integrations, and relates to different goals. Every boundary crossing is a small system transformation.

Sometimes you are so eager to get to the other side that you don't notice what you regret leaving behind. Sometimes you have so much regret that you cannot even look ahead. Sometimes the boundary is so easy that you hardly notice that you have a conflict at all. Sometimes boundaries are so difficult that you do not even recognize that it has become a barrier and believe that there is no other context for experience than the one that you are in, just like Sartre's play, "No Exit".

The prison of a barrier experience is the inability to see things from more than one context. This is what happens when the only way a person can experience is to take it personally.

Every constructed reality is like a map of life. As with all maps, no sooner has it been made than it has to be updated to reflect life's changes. When boundaries are permeable, then the map can be revised as people explore their experience. When boundaries are barriers, then experience is revised to fit the map. This is of course why, in the hierarchy of defense analysis in the systems-centered method, undoing constructed reality comes first.

The first context for undoing mind reading or negative predictions is within the self-system. Crossing from the past into the present, from the future into the present, and exploring reality in the systems-centered role is the primary work of a systems-centered member. The person who is imprisoned by cognitive defenses does not have energy available to do any work until they have undone the defense which keeps them living in the constructed reality of their thoughts.

Structure

Systems-centered leaders define system structure in terms of boundaries. Boundaries in space and time make the difference between whether a systems-centered member, a subgroup or the group-as-a-whole actually exists in the real world or whether they exist only in the mind; whether the work energy is contained and directed towards the goal or whether it is dissipated. For example, a group that keeps a time boundary and starts and stops on time is a very different system from one that does not. A group that contains all its work energy within its boundaries for the duration of its working time, without distractions and irrelevancies drawing the energy away into nostalgia for the past or negative predictions about the future, will have a different quality of work life and a different potential for reaching its goals than one that does not. It will also have a different climate and a different morale.

Boundaries are particularly important when therapy groups are located in clinic or hospital settings. Boundaries that are "impermeable" to irrelevant interruptions during group time make a great difference to how the work energy of the system remains connected to the work. Boundaries that are so permeable that the internal working organization of the system can be disrupted unpredictably and frequently, by phone calls or "crises" from the outside, or competing clinical appointments for the members of the group, "leak" out the energy that is required for the work.

There is another kind of boundary permeability that results in the loss of work energy that is more easily recognized if one thinks about boundaries from a systems perspective. Systems boundaries exist in space and time—they mark the thresholds between the outside and the inside, the past and the future and the present, between fantasy and reality. Inappropriate diversions into anecdotes or gossip about the world outside, diversions into how much better it was in the past, or how things won't work so well in the future, or constructing a view of the group based on negative predictions and fears, not only leak energy across the boundaries away from the here-and-now task, but also leave less and less room for testing out the realities of work.

Once again, the way the people on the team work will have more to do with the context of their work—more to do with the morale and the climate and the way the boundaries are managed, than it will with the people themselves. Who anyone is at any one time has more to do with the way the working system is than who they "are".

Deliberately influencing the way boundaries are managed in space and time is less difficult to do if the structural framework is kept in mind. The same is true for managing the boundary permeability between the system and its environment and the system and its sub-systems. A systems-centered orientation to managing boundaries often makes the difference between a working system that relates to its work goals, and a system that is related to other goals, like safety or survival or status or inertia or sabotage.

There are many systems-centered methods for managing boundaries. Most of the methods are simple to understand and apply, whereas their effect is often complex and far-reaching. Both the method of functional subgrouping and the methods by which restraining forces are deliberately reduced are examples of how understanding function, from the perspective of a theory of living human systems, has been put into practice.

Being able to define the systems structure in terms of its boundaries is a fundamental asset in systems-centered thinking. When this is applied practically in a therapy group, the therapist notes the recognizable set of behaviors that define the role structure of the system and relate the system to the goal. All systems have a specific role in the hierarchy of living systems, and whereas the primary goals are always the same, the secondary goals are almost always different. A systems-centered therapist recognizes the role function by observing how the behavior of the system relates to the goal: either the goal that has been explicitly stated (like, for example, the role system of leader) or the goal that is implied by the way the system is behaving (for example, the role of the systems-centered member crossing the boundary from the self-system into the group-as-a-whole, or the role of the functional subgroup as it relates to the goals of the group-as-a-whole).

Parenthetically, it is the relationship between the behaviors that structure the role and the function of those behaviors as they relate to the goal that makes the force field such a useful tool. Diagnosing a force field of behaviors in the working context will diagnose the balance between the life force and the forces that restrain or impede it (Agazarian, 1986). Once one has learned to think this way, it becomes easier to target interventions by recognizing which restraining forces will make the most difference to the overall change in the hierarchy if they are reduced.

For example, when the anxiety, tension and irritability that frustration at a boundary engenders is defended against, one gets negative predictions and mind reading; aches, pains and psychosomatic symptoms; and depressions and outrages. These are all the "role behaviors" of the defended self-system which play a role in managing frustration, at the expense of the drive of the life force contained in the spontaneous, undefended self. By deliberately weakening these restraining forces through the systematic application of the hierarchy of defense analysis, the defended, false self-role system is weakened, and the role system of the life force becomes the driving force.

Function

Thinking function in systems-centered leadership means thinking about how the system does what it does and how to influence what it does so that it does it more efficiently in relationship to the goal. In other words, how can the systems-centered leader influence the dynamics of function so that the energy of the system is vectored towards the goals?

Systems-centered leaders deliberately influence the way the system functions by influencing the way the energy in the system is organized and directed—in other words, by influencing the way the people in the system behave. The major focus of influence is on the communication behavior that crosses the boundaries (Shannon & Weaver, 1964). At every boundary, the problem has to be solved of what to communicate and how to communicate in order to get the message across.

Systems-centered therapists increase the probability that information will be directed towards solving problems and directed towards organizational goals, not only by monitoring what people communicate but also by establishing communication patterns that are lower on ambiguities, redundancies and contradictions. In other words, for systems-centered therapists, how something is communicated is at least as important as what is communicated, and at times, more important!

In systems-centered thinking, directing communication energy requires keeping the goal of the system in reality focus at all times so that all communications in the systems are related to the goal. It is a small thing to keep the group in mind of the group goal and how much time there is left to reach it, and it makes a big difference (Raven & Rietsema, 1960). Directing communication energy also requires reducing the communications that are not relevant to the goals (Agazarian, 1992). Speed of communication is managed by reducing the kinds of communications that are likely to reduce the probability that the information within the communication will be received. In practice, this can be as simple as deciphering "yes, but", shifting from vague to specific, or requiring a direct rather than an oblique answer to a question.

Systems-centered therapists rely on some form of communication training to manage this. One such tool is the SAVI observation system developed from Information Theory which serves as a map for determining the patterns of communication and their different potentials for making problems or solving them (Simon & Agazarian, 1967). Another tool which is available to systems-centered leaders is the Force Field (Lewin, 1951). The Force Field is a simple way of organizing complex phenomenon so that the restraining forces that are easiest to reduce can be identified and weakened, with the understanding that it is more efficient to solve the problems that lie in the way of the goal than it is to increase the pressure towards the goal (Howard & Scott, 1965).

These are the tools that influence the "function" of the communication as it crosses the boundaries between, within and among systems in the hierarchy. As all systems exist in the environment of the system above them and are the environment of the systems below them, every communication that is sent out of a system will affect the environment of the organization which in turn will affect the systems that take it in.

There is one last principle that is fundamental to systems-centered management and that is the principle of function that is defined for all living human systems. One theory of living human systems states that all systems survive, develop, mature and transform through their ability to recognize and integrate differences: to discriminate that which is different in what is apparently similar and to discriminate that which is similar in what is apparently different.

This is essentially a communication process which depends upon taking in information across the boundaries, integrating what is sufficiently similar, and either storing what is too different in a containing subsystem with permeable boundaries until the system-as-a-whole has developed the ability to integrate it, or rejecting the differences and storing them separately in systems with impermeable boundaries. Systems that have impermeable boundaries tend to stereotype or ghettoize differences which leads to maintaining the hierarchical status quo. Learning how to recognize and integrate differences leads to organizational change. All living human systems require both stability and change if they are to survive, develop and organize. Survival and development depends upon this single process of recognizing and integrating differences over time. The systems-centered approach manages this process through deliberately interfering with the tendency to form stereotype subgroups around similarities and introducing functional subgrouping instead. Functional subgrouping manages the change process by splitting and containing differences in separate subgroups on the one hand, which then function to develop an increasing ability to integrate differences on the other.

Communication

Communicating across every boundary requires sending a message from one place to another. Every communication contains an aspect of the message that is familiar and can be integrated easily into understanding it as it exists. Every communication also contains information that is less familiar or even unfamiliar. Integrating unfamiliar information is not so simple.

All human organizations tend to maintain an existing integration or organization that works to accept similarities and to reject differences. Every difference threatens the status quo. At the same time, organizations survive, develop and transform from simple to complex through their ability to accept and integrate the differences that reflect the needs of changing times and to reject the differences that do not.

Systems-centered therapists therefore pay fundamental attention to the response to differences in the group. The problem to be solved is how to interfere with the natural tendency to fight off differences. For example, the typical response to anything new is an immediate "yes, but ..." Technically this requires a method that stops the natural tendency to close out differences in order to maintain the status quo, and at the same time to increase the tolerance for differences so differences become a resource in problem-solving instead of a threat. Functional subgrouping is the method that systems-centered managers use to address this.

Functional subgrouping

The method of functional subgrouping was developed in the process of putting theory into practice. For example, it can be seen that all living human systems tend to come together and join around similarities and to split and separate around differences. Once this process is completed, differences are typically kept in their place by stereotyping—and stereotype subgroups are formed. It can also be seen that living human systems have a greater tolerance for differences within what is already acceptably similar than they do for similarities in what is already unacceptably different.

Functional subgrouping capitalizes on these two predispositions. Before the system can split around differences, the systems-centered therapist deliberately interferes with the process: deliberately splits the conflicts between two functional subgroups. The functional subgroups come together on their agreements and "contain" the two different halves of the disagreement separately between them while the work group-as-a-whole contains the split. In other words, the "yes, but" is taken out of the individual and contained in the work group.

Any "yes, but" conflict, however small, is a signal to subgroup. The information that is contained in the "yes" is just as important as the information contained in the "but"—and much of the information is likely to be lost if it remains contained in a concealed "yes, but" conflict. Hence, functional subgrouping. In functional subgrouping, one subgroup is encouraged to explore the many meanings of "yes" and the other to explore the many meanings of "but". As both subgroups come together around similarities, each provides a supportive climate. As similarities are explored, so differences in the apparently similar are recognized—a process which develops both differentiation and increased integration of the system. As each subgroup becomes increasingly differentiated, so similarities in what was so apparently different between subgroups are recognized. The end of the process of functional subgrouping is an integration of the "yes" and the "but" and the conflict that it represented, which in turn leads to an understanding of the function of the conflict for the group-as-a-whole.

Summary

The goal of each and every living human system is to survive, to develop and to influence its environment so that the potential for survival and development is increased. System goals are hierarchical: survival is a necessary (though not sufficient) condition for development which is a necessary (though not sufficient) condition for influencing the environment.

Each and every living human system survives, develops and influences its environment through the process of discrimination and integration. Through discriminating differences and integrating them, living human systems transform from simple to complex.

Every system contains its own potential for transformation. How it actualizes its potential determines how it influences the nature of its environment (the living human system above it) and also determines the environmental influence of the system below it. How each and every system actualizes its potential influences the transformation potential of the entire hierarchy of living human systems.

Just as any one system-as-a-whole contains the potential to transform from simple to complex through discrimination and integration, so does the system hierarchy-as-a-whole, and each and every system relationship in it.

The goal of systems-centered change strategy is to make boundaries appropriately permeable to communications between one system and another in the hierarchy of living human systems. This is achieved by reducing the restraining forces to communication at the boundaries.

Techniques for reducing the restraining forces to goal-oriented communications at the boundaries of the system include

- Identifying and working with boundaries.
- Keeping the group work energy focused in the realities of the here-and-now and redirecting it when it takes flight into the past or the future or the irrealities and negative predictions around the present.
- Subgrouping: splitting and containing conflict in the work group rather than in the individual member by splitting the "yes" and the "but" into separate subgroups for exploration.
- Focusing on context rather than content: seeing the problems from different perspectives of the system hierarchy; and understanding the impact of behavior from the perspective of the self-system, the systems-centered member system, the subgroup system, and the system of the group-as-a-whole.
- Differentiating between the exploration and explanation phases of problem-solving and learning to identify and produce the language of exploration and explanation as resources that reach the goal.

The task of systems-centered practice is to bring the work energy into the group-as-a-whole system and direct it towards the system goals, thus enabling the system hierarchy to transform from simple to complex

- To bring the work energy into the group-as-a-whole system by bringing into existence systems-centered member systems, who function to import the work energy across the boundaries of space and time, reality and role.
- To bring the work energy into the group-as-a-whole system by weakening the forces that restrain the work energy from crossing the space boundary from the outside to the inside of the system.

- To bring the work energy into the group-as-a-whole system by weakening the forces that restrain the work energy from crossing the time boundary from the past and future into the present.
- To bring the work energy into the group-as-a-whole system by weakening the forces that restrain the work energy from crossing the role boundary from outside social roles into a systems-centered role of functional subgrouping.
- To bring the work energy into the group-as-a-whole system by weakening the forces that restrain the work energy from crossing the boundary from irreality into the context of the here-and-now as it relates to systems goals of survival, development and environmental mastery and the transformation from simple to complex.

Functional subgrouping

Systems-centered members contain the conflicts encountered along the path to the goal by functional subgrouping. Functional subgrouping manages conflict by splitting differences into like subsystems.

Like subsystems come together around similarities and come to recognize differences in the apparently similar. As differences in the apparently similar are recognized within the subsystems, so similarities in the apparently different are recognized across the subsystems.

The process of **transformation** depends upon system recognition and integration of both similarities and differences: both differences in the apparently similar and similarities in the apparently different.

Because **systems are isomorphic** in structure and function, the process of discrimination and integration is the underlying principle by which the hierarchy of living human systems transforms from simple to complex.

Terminology

There are some additional words in the theory of living human systems that help define the building blocks practically so that they can serve as blueprints for managing change. When systems-centered change is managed within the parameters defined above and operational within the strategies defined below, it can be predicted that change will largely take place in a way that the system-as-a-whole changes in the direction of its goals. These words are:

- **Vectors:** defining the target and amount of energy to be applied to the goals of change.
- **Boundaries:** keeping focused on the here-and-now.
- **Context:** predicting the impact of change from different perspectives of different levels in the organizational hierarchy.
- **Driving and Restraining Forces:** deliberately weakening the restraining forces at the boundaries involved in the change process.
- **Communication as Energy:** reducing the loss of energy in communication due to ambiguities, contradictions and redundancies in the message.
- **Splitting the Conflict:** splitting the conflict between the "yes" and the "but" so that the issues in both sides of the fork-in-the-road between the yes and the but can be explored in functional subgroups.
- **Subgrouping:** using the technique of functional subgrouping so that work teams can join around similarities instead of separating around differences.
- **Stereotype Subgrouping:** functional subgrouping flies in the face of the typical tendency to split around differences and come together around the splits thus creating stereotype subgroups.
- **Functional Subgrouping:** by requiring subgroups to come together around similarities, when differences emerge they are more likely to be tolerated than attacked. In this way, a lot of differentiation can be explored without making too many waves. Then as the differences become recognized in what was apparently similar within each subgroup, the similarities become apparent between each subgroup. In this way, the two subgroups work down to what is common in the conflict that can serve as a platform for resolution rather than getting stuck in the never-ending conflict of the "yes" and the "but".
- **Functional vs. Stereotype Communication:** functional communication uses problem-solving language and methods and can lead to system change. Stereotype communications lead to stereotype problem-solving that maintains the status quo.

- **Common Sense:** crossing the boundaries between comprehension, apprehension and reality.
- **Setting Norms of Communication:** by reducing the ambiguities, redundancies and contradictions within the message.

References

Agazarian, Y. M. (1986). Application of Lewin's life space concept to the individual and group-as-a-whole systems in group psychotherapy. In Stivers, E. & Wheelan, S. (Eds.), *The Lewin legacy* (pp. 101–112). New York: Springer-Verlag.

Agazarian, Y. M. (1991). Systems theory and group psychotherapy: From there-and-then to here-and-now. *The International Forum of Group Psychotherapy, 1*(3).

Agazarian, Y. M. (1992). Contemporary theories of group psychotherapy: A systems approach to the group-as-a-whole. *International Journal of Group Psychotherapy, 42*(3), 177–203.

Bennis, W. G. & Shepard, H. A. (1956). A theory of group development. *Human Relations, 9*(4), 415–437.

Bertalanffy, L. von (1969). *General systems* (revised edition). New York: George Braziller.

Durkin, J. E. (1981). *Living groups: Group psychotherapy and general systems theory.* New York: Brunner/Mazel.

Howard, A. & Scott, R. A. (1965). A proposed framework for the analysis of stress in the human organism. *Journal of Applied Behavioral Science, 10,* 141–160.

Lewin, K. (1951). *Field theory in social science.* New York: Harper & Row.

Raven, B. H. & Rietsema, J. (1960). The effects of varied clarity of group goal and group path upon the individual and his relation to his group. In Cartwright, D. & Zander, A. (Eds.), *Group dynamics research and theory* (2nd ed.). New York: Elmsford, Row, Peterson & Co.

Shannon, C. E. & Weaver, W. (1964). *The mathematical theory of communication.* Urbana, IL: University of Illinois Press.

Simon, A. & Agazarian, Y. M. (1967). *S.A.V.I.: Sequential analysis of verbal interaction.* Philadelphia: Research for Better Schools.

YVONNE AGAZARIAN: BIBLIOGRAPHY

Agazarian, Y. M. (1968). *A theory of verbal behavior and information transfer.* Unpublished doctoral dissertation, Temple University, Philadelphia, PA.

Agazarian, Y. M. (1969). A theory of verbal behavior and information transfer. *Classroom Interaction Newsletter, 4*(2), 22–33.

Agazarian, Y. M. (1969). The agency as a change agent. In Goldberg, M. H. (Ed.), *Blindness research: The expanding frontiers.* University Park, PA: Pennsylvania State University Press.

Agazarian, Y. M. (1972). A system for analyzing verbal behavior (SAVI) applied to staff training in Milieu treatment. *Devereux Schools Forum, 1*(1), 1–32.

Agazarian, Y. M. (1972). Communication through the group process: An approach to humanization. *The Devereux Papers, 1*(1). Philadelphia: The Devereux Forum Press.

Agazarian, Y. M. (1982). Role as a bridge construct in understanding the relationship between the individual and group. In Pines, M. & Rafaelson, L. (Eds.), *The individual and the group, boundaries and inter-relations, Vol. I, Theory.* New York: Plenum Press.

Agazarian, Y. M. (1983). Theory of invisible group applied to individual and group-as-a-whole interpretations. *Group: The Journal of the Eastern Group Psychotherapy Society, 7*(2), 27–37.

Agazarian, Y. M. (1983). Some advantages of applying multi-dimensional thinking to the teaching, practice and outcomes of group psychotherapy. *International Journal of Group Psychotherapy, 33*(2).

Agazarian, Y. M. (1986). Application of Lewin's life space concept to the individual and group-as-a-whole systems in group psychotherapy. In Stivers, E. & Wheelan, S. (Eds.), *The Lewin legacy* (pp. 101–112). New York: Springer-Verlag.

Agazarian, Y. M. (1987). The difficult patient, the difficult group. In Symposium: A discussion of the videotapes of a difficult group. *Group: The Journal of the Eastern Group Psychotherapy Society, 2*(4), 205–216.

Agazarian, Y. M. (1988). *Application of a modified force field analysis to the diagnosis of implicit group goals.* Paper presented at the Third International Kurt Lewin Conference of the Society for the Advancement of Field Theory.

Agazarian, Y. M. (1989). Group-as-a-whole systems theory and practice. *Group: The Journal of the Eastern Group Psychotherapy Society, 13*(3–4), 131–155.

Agazarian, Y. M. (1989). The invisible group: An integrational theory of group-as-a-whole. The 12th Annual Foulkes Memorial Lecture. *Group Analysis, 22*(4), 74–96.

Agazarian, Y. M. (1989, February). *Pathogenic beliefs and implicit goals: Discussion of "The Mount Zion group: The therapeutic process and applicability of the group's work to psychotherapy".* Paper presented at the Slavson Memorial Lecture, American Group Psychotherapy Association Annual Meeting, San Francisco.

Agazarian, Y. M. (1991). Discussion of "Group Disjunction" by Charlotte Hahn from a systems-centered perspective. *Journal of Psychoanalysis and Psychotherapy, 9*(2), 162–167.

Agazarian, Y. M. (1991). The systems-centered perspective: Discussion of "Idealization and Omnipotence within the Group Matrix" by Keith Hyde. *Group Analysis, 24*(3), 279–297.

Agazarian, Y. M. (1991). Systems theory and group psychotherapy: From there-and-then to here-and-now. *The International Forum of Group Psychotherapy, 1*(3).

Agazarian, Y. M. (1992). Contemporary theories of group psychotherapy: A systems approach to the group-as-a-whole. *International Journal of Group Psychotherapy, 42*(3), 177–203.

Agazarian, Y. M. (1992). Book review. [Review of the book *Koinonia: From hate, through dialogue, to culture in the large group,* by de Mare, P.]. *International Journal of Group Psychotherapy, 42*(3).

Agazarian, Y. M. (1992, February). *The use of two observation systems to analyze the communication patterns in two videotapes of the interpersonal approach to group psychotherapy.* [Based on Yalom, I.D. "Understanding group psychotherapy" (videotape). Pacific Grove, CA: Brooks-Cole.] Panel on "Contrasting views of representative group events," American Group Psychotherapy Association Annual Meeting, New Orleans.

Agazarian, Y. M. (1993). Reframing the group-as-a-whole. In Hugg, T. Carson, N. & Lipgar, R. (Eds.), *Changing group relations: Proceedings of the ninth scientific meeting of the A.K. Rice Institute* (pp. 165–187). Juniper, FL: A.K.R.I. Institute.

Agazarian, Y. M. (1994). The phases of development and the systems-centered group. In Pines, M. & Schermer, V. (Eds.), *Ring of fire: Primitive object relations and affect in group psychotherapy* (pp. 36–85). London: Routledge, Chapman & Hall.

Agazarian, Y. M. (1996). An-up-to-date guide to the theory, constructs and hypotheses of a theory of living human systems and its systems-centered practice. *SCT Journal: Systems-Centered Theory and Practice,* 1(1), 3–12.

Agazarian, Y. M. (1996). Systems-centered therapy applied to short-term group and individual psychotherapy. *SCT Journal: Systems-Centered Theory and Practice,* 1(1), 23–34.

Agazarian, Y. M. (1997). Glossary of SCT terms. *SCT Journal: Systems-Centered Theory and Practice,* 2(1), 3–10.

Agazarian, Y. M. (1997). *Systems-centered therapy for groups.* New York: Guilford Press. Re-printed in paperback (2004). London: Karnac Books.

Agazarian, Y. M. (1999). Systems-centered therapy. In Donigian, J. & Hulse-Killacky, D. *Critical incidents in group therapy.* Belmont, CA: Wadsworth Publishing Co.

Agazarian, Y. M. (1999). Phases of development in the systems-centered group. *Small Group Research,* 30(1), 82–107.

Agazarian, Y. M. (1999). Systems-centered supervision. *International Journal of Group Psychotherapy,* 49(2), 215–236.

Agazarian, Y. M. (1999). Systems-centered therapy. In Rosenthal, H.G. (Ed.), *Favorite counseling and therapy techniques.* Washington, DC: Accelerated Development.

Agazarian, Y. M. (1999). Response to Wright's review of "Systems-Centered Therapy for Groups." *International Journal of Group Psychotherapy,* 49(2).

Agazarian, Y. M. (2000). *The language of functional subgrouping.* Philadelphia: Good Enough Press.

Agazarian, Y. M. (2001). *A systems-centered approach to inpatient group psychotherapy.* London and Philadelphia: Jessica Kingsley.

Agazarian, Y. M. (2001). Systemzentrierte gruppenpsychotherapie—Konzepte der theorie lebender menschlicher systeme. In Tschuschke, V. (Ed.), *Praxes der gruppenpsychotherapie*. Stuttgart: Georg Thieme Verlag.

Agazarian, Y. M. (2001). Siblings in beeld. *Groeps Psychotherapie, 35*(1).

Agazarian, Y.M. (2002). A systems-centered approach to individual and group psychotherapy. In Vandecreek, L. & Jackson, T. (Eds.), *Innovations in clinical practice: A source book, Vol. 20* (pp. 223–240). Sarasota, FL: Professional Resource Press.

Agazarian, Y. M. (2003). Book review. [Review of the book *Traumatic experience in the unconscious life of groups*, by Hopper, E.]. In *Systems-Centered Training News, 11*(1), 3–4.

Agazarian, Y. M. (2006). *Systems centered practice: Selected papers on group psychotherapy*. London: Karnac Books.

Agazarian, Y. M. (1995/2010). Five papers from the Friends Hospital training series: Fall 1992—Fall 1995. In Carter, F. Lum, K. Peightel, J. Robbins, M. Silverstein, M. Vadell, J. Viskari, S. E. (Eds.), *Systems-centered theory and practice: The contribution of Yvonne Agazarian* (pp. 1–46). Livermore, CA: WingSpan Press. (Previously unpublished papers)

Agazarian, Y. M., Boyer, G. E., Simon, A. & White, P. F. (Eds.) (1973). *Documenting development*. Philadelphia: Research for Better Schools.

Agazarian, Y. M. & Byram, C. (2009). First build the system: The systems-centered approach to combined psychotherapy. *Group: The Journal of the Eastern Group Psychotherapy Society, 33*(2), 129–148.

Agazarian, Y. M. & Carter, F. (1993). Discussions on the large group. *Group: The Journal of the Eastern Group Psychotherapy Society, 17*(4), 210–234.

Agazarian, Y. M. & Gantt, S. P. (2000). *Autobiography of a theory*. London: Jessica Kingsley.

Agazarian, Y. M. & Gantt, S. P. (2003). Phases of group development: Systems-centered hypotheses and their implications for research and practice. *Group Dynamics: Theory, Research and Practice, 7*(3), 238–252.

Agazarian, Y. M. & Gantt, S. P. (2005). The systems perspective. In Wheelan, S. (Ed.), *Handbook of group research and practice*. Thousand Oaks, CA: Sage Publications.

Agazarian, Y. M. & Gantt, S. P. (2005). The systems-centered approach to the group-as-a-whole. *Group: The Journal of the Eastern Group Psychotherapy Society, 29*(1), 163–186.

Agazarian, Y. M. & Janoff, S. (1993). Systems theory and small groups. In. Kaplan, I & Sadock, B. (Eds.), *Comprehensive textbook of group psychotherapy* (pp. 33–44, 3rd ed.). Maryland: Williams & Wilkins, Division of Waverly.

Agazarian, Y. M. & Peters, R. (1981). *The visible and invisible group.* London: Routledge & Kegan Paul, Ltd. Re-printed in paperback (1987). London: Karnac Books.

Agazarian, Y. M. & Philibossian, B. (1998). A theory of living human systems as an approach to leadership of the future with examples of how it works. In Klein, E. Gabelnick, F. & Herr, P. (Eds.), *The psychodynamics of leadership* (pp. 127–160). Madison, CT: Psychosocial Press.

Gantt, S. P. & Agazarian, Y. M. (2004). Systems-centered emotional intelligence: Beyond individual systems to organizational systems. *Organizational Analysis, 12*(2), 147–169.

Gantt, S. P. & Agazarian, Y. M. (Eds.) (2005). *SCT in action: Applying the systems-centered approach in organizations.* Lincoln, NE: iUniverse. Reprint (2006). London: Karnac Books.

Gantt, S. P. & Agazarian, Y. M. (Eds.) (2006). *SCT in clinical practice: Applying the systems-centered approach with individuals, families and groups.* Livermore, CA: WingSpan Press.

Gantt, S. P. & Agazarian, Y. M. (2007). Phases of system development in organizational work groups: The systems-centered approach for intervening in context. *Organisational & Social Dynamics, 7*(2), 253–291.

Ladden, L., Gantt, S. P., Rude, S. & Agazarian, Y. M. (2007). Systems-centered therapy: A protocol for treating generalized anxiety disorder. *Journal of Contemporary Psychotherapy. 37*(2), 61–70.

Simon, A. & Agazarian, Y. M. (1967). *S.A.V.I.: Sequential analysis of verbal interaction.* Philadelphia: Research for Better Schools.

Simon, A. & Agazarian, Y. M. (2000). The system for analyzing verbal interaction. In Beck, A. & Lewis, C. (Eds.), *The process of group psychotherapy: Systems for analyzing change.* Washington, D.C.: American Psychological Association.

Simon, A. & Agazarian, Y. M. (2000). SAVI: Theory and applications of the system for analyzing verbal interaction. In Beck, A. Greene, L. & Lewis, C. (Eds.), *Process in therapeutic groups: A handbook of systems of analysis.* New York: Guilford Press.

CHAPTER TWO

The radical innovation of subgroups

Kenneth Eisold, Ph.D.

It is virtually axiomatic in our culture that groups are composed of individuals. If we ask how large a group is or how best to characterize it, we are surely thinking about the specific members that, we assume, make the group what it is. Other cultures, less focused on individuals and their differences, may have other ways of thinking about this, but this is our way.

Yet this way of thinking inevitably gives rise to a series of conflicts and dilemmas for those entering groups. How much of themselves will they have to give up to become members? What compromises will they have to make? What identities or characteristics will they be forced to assume in order to fit in? What other members will be competing for leadership and recognition? Who else is likely to grab the limited attention available? Who is likely to dominate? And then there are those who always seem to oppose group decisions, or just go on talking endlessly. What members will be marginalized, neglected? What members will come out on top?

These seemingly inevitable dilemmas and conflicts give groups in our culture a somewhat negative cast. If decisions have to be made or actions taken, we try to think of some way to navigate around the groups that need to be involved. We tend to believe groups stand in the way, that they block actions, obscure issues. As individuals we feel free, as group members we are constrained, forced to conform.

Moreover, we are aware of the danger of "Groupthink", the unconsciously coercive power of groups to limit and distort our thinking. The need of individuals to protect their distinctive identities exerts an insidious demand on group members to get along with each other. At the very least, it makes it difficult to take unpopular positions or to mention inconvenient facts.

On the other hand, many of us know that groups can be more powerful and effective than individuals. The collection of abilities and skills gathered together in groups can add immeasurably to our thinking. Moreover, their synergistic interactions can produce effects way beyond what individuals achieve alone. Nonetheless, faced with bringing up an issue before a committee or a board, our usual attitude is some version of dread.

Yvonne Agazarian writes about a moment in the early development of her thinking when she suddenly saw that our culture promotes the belief that we are the center of the world: "I then hypothesized that this unconscious pathogenic belief is acted out, in both individual and group therapy, by treating the patient as if he or she is the center of the world and that the patient is thus unconsciously encouraged to take things personally" (Agazarian, 1997). Systems-centered thinking was her way out of this dilemma. Functional subgrouping was the technique that made it possible for groups to work more effectively.

As I see it, subgrouping started out as a discovery: we are not at the center of our worlds. As group members, we are inevitably allied with others, embedded in subgroups of like-minded members. Groups are constantly shifting arrays of subgroups, our memberships usually unconsciously determined by our needs for understanding and affiliation. Whatever action the group-as-a-whole takes, or does not take, is the product of all the subgroup vectors that combine to produce that final result.

But, then, she transforms this discovery into a method for working in groups. SCT pushes these largely unconscious alliances into the forefront, identifies them, and turns them into a way of communicating. If individual group members work to identify the subgroups to which they belong, and if other group members can locate themselves with respect to those and other subgroups, it becomes possible for a dialogue to occur among subgroup members that enlarges and clarifies the nature of what is going on within the group-as-a-whole.

A group member with an issue, whether it is a response to another member, an anxious or hopeless state of mind, an obsessive preoccupation, or a difficulty in joining the work of the group at any given moment, is asked to find the subgroup composed of others who share that issue. As the subgroup forms, the issue becomes de-centered from the particular person who introduced it, explored as an aspect of the system within which it has arisen. The exploration of similarities within subgroups inevitably leads to greater understanding about the issue and greater clarity about its meaning for the system. Inevitably that also leads to further differentiation, as members of the subgroup begin to discriminate different aspects of the issue that connects them. Gradually, then, subgroups reform around the newly emergent differences, and the identification of new issues leads to the formation of new subgroups, as the system moves on.

This process of "functional subgrouping" is dialectical. Problems are not "solved", dealt with or disposed of, but rather transformed as a by-product of the system's continuing process of adaptation. And along the way, personal meanings become less relevant to the group process. Functional subgrouping moves the issue away from personal exploration or individual historical meaning, as the person has moved on from being "self-centered" to "system-centered".

Let me stop here with my account of this process, because I am now infringing on matters that Yvonne Agazarian has described so much better than I possibly can. My point is not about how to facilitate this process, but simply to note its radical implications. If the basic building blocks of groups are subgroups, not individual members, then not only do we all possess a new concept to help make groups more effective, countering our cultural prejudices about group processes, but we also have a new and radical understanding of what it means to be a group member.

I write this largely as an observer and relative outsider. I am not a licensed SCT practitioner or trainee. My knowledge of it comes from having attended a weekend workshop as well as observing several demonstration groups at the American Group Psychotherapy Association's (AGPA) annual conference. More importantly, it comes from having consulted to the Board of SCTRI over the past 15 years or more as it has worked to develop its management structure. Meeting twice yearly, the Board employs SCT techniques, including functional subgrouping, to conduct its discussions and resolve its differences—and for me that has been a privileged window into seeing the concepts employed by those who know them best.

My own training in group processes came from Group Relations, with its focus on the group-as-a-whole and authority relationships. No doubt I have seen subgrouping at work many times over the years, though it was not part of my conceptual framework at the start. Now, however, it strikes me that understanding subgrouping adds a vital dimension to grasping group process, one that could easily be integrated into traditional group relations work. Indeed, I believe it would immeasurably enrich it.

I have also been trained as a psychoanalyst, and that has helped me to focus on a related discovery about the subject, the individual self, that is more implicit in SCT but every bit as radical as the discovery about subgroups. The awareness of individuals as continuously shifting and changing parts of the systems they inhabit, forming and re-forming subgroups, implies a new understanding of the self. What does it say about us as distinct persons that we are able to form subgroups so readily and combine with others so fluidly, shifting into new subgroups as the process evolves? What holds us together or forms our identity? What does it mean to have a self?[1]

Developmental psychology has taught us that there is a critical moment when young children first realize they are somebody. They come to grasp that just as the word "dog" refers to the four-legged pet that barks, "I" refers to the unique person who has their name and lives in their body, a self that is like other selves, but also separate and different. "I am 'me'. I am someone too".

We view this experience as indispensable to our psychological and moral development. It prepares us to develop a sense of agency, which in turn is essential for assuming responsibility. Without believing one is a distinct self, one cannot be truly accountable for what one does. It is important, then, to understand our separateness and to disengage from our need to rely on others, to act on our own behalf. But our contemporary culture encourages us to hold on, tenaciously, to that infantile sense of our own unique importance.

For us, that childhood experience of possessing a "self" has become the basis for our reigning concept of what it means to be a human being.

Our concept of the "self" denotes a container that holds everything belonging to us, the organs bounded by our skin, the thoughts inside our minds. From this point of view, we speak of "ourselves", "myself", "himself", and so on. Our selves belong to us—as do their contents. This is why the discovery of the self in young children is of such central importance. They grasp for the first time that they are not the possession of anyone else; they assert ownership over their bodies and their thoughts, their feelings and their intentions.

Over time, experience teaches that this possession is partial and provisional. As we mature, we learn that to insist upon one's autonomy and independence can become impoverishing. But this is where we start to become responsible agents and assemble our cultural identities.

William James took this idea of the self as his point of departure: *"In its widest possible sense ... a man's Self is the sum total of all that he CAN call his, not only his body and his psychic powers, but his clothes and his house, his wife and children, his ancestors and friends, his reputation and works, his lands and horses ... "*[2] (James, 1890, vol. 1, p. 291). This generous and expansive definition bears the earmarks of James' historical moment, of course: today, in an age where women have at least legal grounds for claiming full social and economic equality, few men would risk referring to their wives as a part of themselves. But all definitions are historically bound, reflecting the fact that our thinking emerges from a particular social context. This is especially true of the "self".

The concept of the "self" could only begin to emerge in our history when the idea of possession became central to our common experience and the acquisition of possessions became an important social focus. The importance of possessions, in turn, depended upon a significantly increased social mobility. Those who did not have wealth and status conferred upon them by birth sought the opportunities to acquire them in order to take their place in the world, to become somebody. These developments overlapped with what is often referred to as the "rise of individualism", the idea that each person in society had inalienable rights as well as independent economic interests. Throughout the eighteenth century, society came to be seen as arising out of a consensual contract of free men, and the growth of the economy, the wealth of nations, was attributed to unfettered competition among free agents.

My point is that the self is an important social concept that did much to emancipate citizens from the traditional order of society. As distinct and separate selves, we gradually became free to assemble into larger social units, to select the leaders and governments we wanted, and to assume a greater degree of control over our lives. But while it has freed us from traditional restraints, it has not told us much about who we are.

Many of us in the modern world, faced with a defining concept of ourselves as a container, have resorted to the belief that at the core of the self must be something that possesses the self itself, an original source, an essence.[3] The self has come to seem something like the secular version of the soul, a precious and unique primal gift. But there is little evidence for this, and philosophers, by and large, give this idea little credence.

In fact, our culture today appears to have reached a kind of crisis as the container of the "self" spills over its expanded boundaries or even breaks up under the stress of its own demands. The burgeoning psychotherapy industry caters to clients who feel themselves to be fragmented or depleted, inadequate or self-deprecating. Narcissism presents selves with inflated self-esteem, while, on the other hand, depression arises in selves that are neglected or insufficiently appreciated. The middle ground is not only difficult to establish but difficult to locate. What is important about us? What are reasonable expectations and normal desires? Self-esteem seems to be required, but can narcissism also be essential to our well-being? The importance of the self is widely acknowledged, its defects and ills frequently discussed, but today it cannot be defined with much specificity, nor can we assert with any confidence a curative process or an ideal state to strive for. In a culture grounded in competition and boundless ambition, there can be little lasting agreement on such questions.

This lengthy excursion is designed to bring home that one of the great strengths of SCT, seldom explicitly noted, is that it completely side steps such problems. Being "system-centered", not "self-centered", it does not concern itself with the isolated and autonomous individual. It brushes past the boundaries of individual selves. The focus on systems illuminates the dynamics of groups, as we have seen. But it may be even more important for providing a critique of our society's preoccupation with the self, the unique individual that we all so easily fall into believing we are—or, worse, think we ought to be.

The system-centered world, then, is not a world of human objects interacting and colliding, but a world of energies merging and diverging, vectoring and differentiating. Yvonne has wisely looked to other disciplines for alternatives to the conventional Newtonian world of objects. Years ago, she focused on Shannon's (1948) mathematical theory of Communication to express the dynamic properties of interaction and flow. More recently, she has expressed interest in the findings of Complexity Theory (personal communication, 2009) to express how order and structure emerge out of randomness. The point is not so much the need to ground SCT on a new metaphysic as it is to escape from the confines of the old metaphysic that inevitably takes us back to conventional assumptions about a world of objects, including ourselves as discrete selves.

She needed to be free to think of energy as it is actually experienced in our bodies and in our group and subgroup interactions. That energy may be easy to feel and to describe, but it is not easy to theorize about as Freud himself found out when he developed his libido theory. He too discovered that it made clinical sense to describe something that one can feel in one's body, and that, moreover, appears to account for actual behavior. And yet, the attempt to theorize libido as a physical reality led Freud and many of the psychoanalysts that followed him into a thicket of problems that, in the end, only served to make psychoanalysis more questionable in the eyes of those who took its scientific pretensions seriously. Yvonne Agazarian has wisely, I think, indicated the presence of the issue of the nature and scientific definition of energy pragmatically, but has not allowed herself to be distracted from the main task of articulating her own theory of behavior. Others, no doubt, in years to come, will take our understanding of this further.

If energy is the key concept that fills in for the large question of the drives, desires, fears, and tropisms that push or pull selves in their interactions with each other, role is the key concept that links behavior to the larger world. And here, she has made significant contributions as well. Almost alone among those who have developed therapeutic approaches to behavior, she has taken seriously the social and organizational context in which that behavior occurs.

Role, in a sense, is where the person and the system meet. The system needs members to take up roles because the system itself needs to adapt to reality, and roles define the functions required for that adaptation. The system needs leaders to take action, thinkers to plan, critics to refine thinking, doers to implement decisions, and so forth. Short of such arrays of functional roles, any system is inert. On the other hand, members need roles in order to realize their own potential and to grow. Roles, in effect, represent the choices that members have for action in the group, and through choosing roles they bring into existence who they can be or need to be at any given moment. We might say that a role is what the self can be in a specific context, for a specific purpose, for a limited time. So when an individual member in a group finds a functional role in a group, he or she is both fulfilling a need in the group to further its work of adaptation and also a personal need to be useful and concretize who he or she can be at that moment. It is a demand on the self to act and to realize its potential for action.

But role means more than a function. As Yvonne Agazarian reminds us, it is also a part in a play. The word derives, in fact, from an old French term, "rolle", referring to the script or role of paper from which an actor read his part. Actors can play many parts, of course, though only one at a time. Similarly, group members can take up different roles, actualizing different parts of themselves at different times. But, inevitably, there will be a part the person feels compelled to play, a part that will feel not so much a function in the service of adaptation but something akin to who they are, who they feel they have to be, and they will try to play it again and again. Such roles usually derive from early childhood and we often tenaciously insist on carrying them out. Moreover, we often find others willing and able to play the complementary roles that enable the entire scene to be enacted. The rebellious son will find a strict father, the dutiful daughter a demanding mother—and so forth.

It is this complexity of roles—simultaneously a function and a part in a play, analogous to an identity—that makes the concept so useful therapeutically. There is the demand of reality to take on a function, important to the survival of the system as a whole, and then there is the pressure in the person to repeat the part he has played again and again. The disparity between the two constitutes the therapeutic leverage of SCT.

Psychoanalysis has a comparable way of viewing this tension, but a different way of processing it. "Transference", the tendency to repeat and reenact old relationships, comes up against the reality of present, real relationships. When the facts of the analyst's actual behavior with the patient do not fit his expectations, the patient has an opportunity to detect his embedded assumptions. The advantage of SCT here is that the reality is being consistently evoked and checked out because role behavior in the group is constantly monitored. The presence of the group means that there is an array of others who are able to play complementary roles, and the focus on subgrouping provides a way to explore similarities and differences so that disparities can be identified and checked out.

These two concepts, energy and role, provide vital flexibility. Energy enables the SCT practitioner to avoid having to define and limit his or her understanding of the person in the group. It makes it possible to focus on the subgrouping activity and deduce from that what stance to take towards the subject. Role enables, on the other hand, a way to evaluate behavior not in personal terms but in terms of the needs of the system. Our capacity to take on a diversity of roles makes us malleable, adaptive. On the other hand, it is our ability to understand and accept the roles we inhabit that make us responsible and effective.

These concepts take us beyond therapy. SCT is Systems-Centered Therapy, of course, and should be. Yvonne Agazarian started as a therapist, and she developed her ideas in that context. Virtually all of those who enter training come from the traditional disciplines of mental health, and they go on to pursue careers as psychotherapists. But the ideas have very broad applicability, and many practitioners are extending it in exciting new ways. As a consultant to the SCTRI Board for many years, I have experienced myself the capacity of the theory to promote productive organizational work. I believe we are on the verge of seeing other applications for these tools of unprecedented flexibility and value.

It is Yvonne Agazarian's triumph to have instituted such a radical change from our conventional assumptions through the work of SCT. No argument needs to be made, no old ideas challenged.

Simply though the inherent logic of the work and the results it produces, we go beyond who we thought we were.

References

Agazarian, Y. M. (1997). *Systems-centered therapy for groups.* New York: Guilford Press.
Eisold, K. (2010). *What you don't know you know.* New York: Other Press.
James, W. (1980). *Principles of psychology,* (vol. 1, p. 291). New York: Henry Holt & Co.
LeDoux, J. (2002). *The synaptic self.* New York: Macmillan.
Shannon, C. E. (1948). A mathematical theory of communication. *The Bell System Technical Journal, 27,* 379–423, 623–656.

Notes

1. For a more extended discussion of the self, as well as other concepts of the individual person, see chapters three and four in Eisold, K., *What You Don't Know You Know* (New York: Other Press, 2010).
2. Joseph LeDoux, citing James, opts for a comparable definition: "In my view, the self is the totality of what an organism is physically, biologically, psychologically, socially and culturally. Though it is a unit, it is not unitary. It includes things that we know and things that we do not know, things that others know about us that we do not realize. It includes features that we express and hide, and some that we simply don't call upon. It includes what we would like to be as well as what we hope we never become". *The Synaptic Self*, p. 31.
3. Clearly, the idea that the self or the mind survives death is based on a belief in an immutable core, but few contemporary philosophers subscribe to an essentialist idea of a self.

CHAPTER THREE

Two perspectives on a trauma in a training group: the systems-centered approach and the theory of incohesion

Susan P. Gantt, Ph.D., ABPP, CGP, FAGPA, FAPA
Earl Hopper, Ph.D., MInstGA, CGP

Along with Yvonne Agazarian, Susan Gantt and Earl Hopper were interested in the similarities and differences between their respective theoretical and clinical approaches. Susan Gantt was working from the point of view of Agazarian's theory of living humans systems (TLHS) and its systems-centered therapy and training (SCT) (Agazarian, 1997) and Earl Hopper from the point of view of group analysis and psychoanalysis. Therefore, Susan and Yvonne made a tentative plan with Earl for him to observe the more advanced of two SCT groups who were meeting concurrently as part of their three-day training event. Unfortunately, we all failed to confirm the plan, and Susan, the leader of the SCT group that was to be observed, did not inform the group that Earl would be observing it. Thus, the group was completely unprepared by Susan for Earl's arrival and his entry into the group's space, and hence quite unconsciously, unintentionally and regrettably, we precipitated a group trauma.

In an attempt to make lemonade from lemons, we decided that actually this offered us a chance to consider this traumatic experience from our respective theoretical and clinical perspectives. This paper, which is an edited and abbreviated version of "Two Perspectives on a Trauma in a Training Group: The Systems-Centered Approach and the Theory of Incohesion" (Gantt & Hopper, 2008a, b), is the product of our discussions. We have tried to convey here a sense of our continuing dialogue.

Earl: Yvonne and I have been friends for many years, and we have many friends in common throughout the world. We have often discussed our ideas about living human systems and the application of these ideas to the work of consultation and psychotherapy, especially group analytic therapy. I am pleased to acknowledge Yvonne's influence on my career and professional development. I am especially pleased that Susan and I have been able to continue working in this personal, intellectual and professional tradition.

Susan: There is no doubt that Yvonne has been the single most important influence on my work. Her theory and methods make intuitive, clinical and theoretical sense to me in a way that no other theory has. I am very pleased here to represent the systems-centered theory and methods that Yvonne has developed, and do hope I do justice to them. And I am very pleased to be engaged in this kind of dialogue with Earl on the occasion of honoring Yvonne's work.

We first present excerpts from the empirical material collected from the group members retrospectively about their experience of the "unexpected" group observation, and then discuss this material from each of the two theoretical perspectives.

The group and its trauma

We start with excerpts from the verbatim descriptions of the trauma from the group members' perspective. The SCT training group was in the last afternoon of a three-day experiential workshop on exploring roles. This group was composed of members at an intermediate level in SCT training. They had mastered taking membership in an SCT group, centering into themselves and their primary experience, using functional subgrouping to explore group conflicts, and modifying the basic defenses that SCT groups undo: cognitive defenses of anxiety, the somatic defenses of tension, and the discharge defenses of depression and outrage that defend against the retaliatory impulse (Agazarian, 1997).

In SCT, centering relates to grounding into one's body and connecting a person to primary apprehensive, sensory experience, with an awareness of both self-experience and context. Working from one's centered experience provides an important platform for exploring the pull into old roles without enacting the role itself. The goal of the group was to explore stereotyped, personalized roles as they were elicited in the group context. The group had identified many roles that were elicited for them in the group and the triggers that stimulated the emergence of these roles. They explored the roles' phenomenology and genetic origins, worked to undo the original splits the old roles maintained, and learned to shift away from the role to discover the primary experience that the role blocked.

With one hour of "small group" work remaining, the observer, Earl, entered. The leader and the group were taken by surprise! The leader, Susan, recovered enough to orient the group to the plan that she and Earl had made for him to observe, and to tell the group that she had "forgotten" to let them know about this. Not surprisingly, therefore, the interruption violated the structure and, simultaneously, the SCT norms of informing a group when they were to be observed. These violations precipitated an "authority issue" with the leader, the SCT term for the negative transference with the leader.

When this subsided, Susan suggested to the group that they explore the impact of the unexpected interruption in the context of roles, which was the focus of the workshop, in particular by noticing what roles and experiences were stimulated by the leader's failing to prepare them for this intrusion by an unexpected observer. The group then explored the roles and role solutions that emerged in the group work following the disruption and failure in leadership.

What happened from the perspective of the participants

Within a few weeks of the group's meeting, Susan wrote to each of the participants asking them to write briefly about their memory of the group session. The group members obliged. Taken together, the responses which are presented below represent the group's response to this failure in leadership and the unexpected break in structure and norms. Obviously, the traumatic nature of this event is not exactly the same as, say, the bombing of Pearl Harbor, but in so far as our theories of the value of training events are valid, this experience of failed dependency and intrusive boundary breaking was certainly traumatic.

The first member. I saw an elderly man come into the room [sic: referring to the unexpected observer, Earl]. I assumed that he was in the wrong place and on realizing this, would leave. As it became apparent that he was coming further into the room, I expected Susan or Tim (pseudonym) would address him, either ask where he was trying to find or ask him to leave the room. [Tim was an advanced trainee who was working in a leadership training role in which his goal was to join subgroups authentically in the service of the development of the group-as-a-whole instead of in the service of his personal learning.] However, he came further into the room and I became increasingly surprised that neither Susan nor Tim appeared to be dealing with the interruption. I think that as he headed for a seat on the far side of the room and had some verbal exchange with Susan about where he should be, she announced that she had forgotten to tell the group that we would be having an observer.

It seemed extraordinary that having an observer could be forgotten and I don't think I really believed that this was what had happened. I felt really angry and assumed that Yvonne [sic: the workshop director and leader of the other training group in the adjoining room] had set this up. I thought she thought that as a (whole) group we had not dealt with the authority issue and had set up the interruption in order to provoke a reaction. I think one of the other members started talking in a furious fashion about some previous contact she had had with Earl, but I think I was probably constructing my own view of what was happening at the time.

My response to "being set up" was one of defiance, thinking "don't think you can make me do what you want me to". This made me not want to verbalize my feeling about the leader (Yvonne).

The mystery man sat behind me and I couldn't see him. I realize now that I had no curiosity about who he was (I didn't know him). Perhaps also because he was out of my line of vision I could in some way "wipe him out". (I had used this expression about the member taking on the leadership training role in a group on the previous day. On that occasion I had been able to wipe him out by keeping him out of my line of vision).

It was rather more difficult to keep the mystery man out of my vision as I became gradually aware that he was making noises, and leaning forward on his chair, and intermittently I could see him in my peripheral vision. This aroused the thought that he was not conducting himself in a manner appropriate to an observer.

The group was disrupted by his entrance. It seemed that we had all been shocked and gone into our person role but gradually we were able to move back into the member role. There was strong support and agreement from the group that we should do this and it really helped. As we took up the member role, we were able to explore the experience. Finally I think the group felt satisfied that we had been able to return to the goal of the work, i.e., to explore roles.

A second member. I don't recall having spoken yet in this group when a man walked into the room. I remember having an impulse to get up and speak to him but, knowing I was not the leader, I looked to Susan. I then looked back at him and heard another member say Earl Hopper's name. I had not recognized him before this, even though I had met him. I also knew about a difficult personal meeting another member had had with Earl in another context.

Susan then said that he was coming to observe us, and I remember thinking how composed Susan looked, as she told us that she had forgotten to tell us. I also felt shocked and incredulous, but did not feel angry. I was aware of my care-taking impulse in relation to Susan.

The group now felt incredibly chaotic and raucous with all the attention shifted from the group and the "hold" of the leader, to the outside of the group on to Earl. Like we had turned inside out. This was made easier by him eating a biscuit, as well as leaning forward into the group, as it seemed at times he was having difficulty hearing.

After some time of the group outraging, I said from my container role that we needed to vector our energy back across the boundary to the work we had started at the beginning of the session. I reminded the group that we had been begun again, to look at the fork between adaptive and maladaptive roles, and we needed to return to that using this to do so. I also asked the group if everyone was centered, and said that we needed to go inside of ourselves for our experience. I felt the group responded and there was some shift. Attention was still towards Earl, but it felt like the experience was more in the group and inside of ourselves than out of the group.

The group continued to explore their experience, with Earl and Susan as the "trigger" to go into role. We subgrouped more strongly now and as the energy came into the group, Susan became the target for the authority issue which had been triggered. This was worked with a bit, but time was a constraint also. It felt like I left the group with unfinished business.

Third participant. What I remember is the door opening and thinking he's got the wrong room and in a minute Susan will say something. This was quickly followed by my feeling of shock as I recognized Earl Hopper and thinking surely he can't be coming into this group. The group sense of shock and disruption as he came in. Exploring our bewilderment and then anger in subgroups. Knowing that my shock came partly from a previous encounter with Earl Hopper and trying to keep my focus on the present. Finding the eye contact very helpful, particularly with two members. Having to work hard at staying focused on our goal of exploring roles and not be drawn into watching Earl Hopper. Feeling angry with the fact that he ate biscuits, rocked on his chair, picked his nose. Thinking he hasn't got the faintest idea of how to be an observer—and saying so to Susan at the end, suggesting it was her responsibility to coach him in his role. Realizing this was a great opportunity to explore not going into my "rabbit in the headlights role". Feeling slightly hysterical and laughing with others at the absurdity of the situation. Images of powerful people and statues (Boudicca sticks out). Expressing our anger towards Susan. Taking charge of ourselves and our goal and a sense of Susan only being in the background. Very strong sense of the subgrouping supporting us and the group supporting its members. Feeling at the end that we had sat in the fire and come out transformed and stronger.

Fourth participant. When Earl entered the room I had mostly curiosity. I did become more self-conscious. However, it was more excitement than anxiety. Actually, I was excited to "show off". As I worked in the group, I started to perceive differences between myself and the group members who were having a more aversive response. I tried to stay empathic by thinking about how I could feel if "triggered" by someone who came into the group unannounced.

As I write this, I realize that I became much more self-conscious, started to lose a systems perspective, went into my head, and became somewhat alienated from the group. I then had the impulse to: 1) join a subgroup even if I was not resonating with a subgroup; and 2) target the visitor whom I started to judge (e.g., What a jerk.

Look at his posture. The guy is totally defensive. He thinks he is better than us, etc.). However, I am not sure of the chronology of events. Bottom line is that I did not have a strong reaction that I was aware of, judged myself, made inauthentic attempts to join a subgroup versus staying with the fact that I really was not too sure about what my experience was, then admitting to the subgroup that I was not really in it. All of that opposed to staying curious about my reaction and keeping a systems perspective in mind.

Fifth member. The work we did in the group exploring the roles we go into was extremely valuable and I feel it has shifted something in myself. The cognitive understanding of a role has really given me a sense of "identity" of the roles (or at least one!) I have. This makes it much easier to understand it from all perspectives and begin to make changes. Because of the work we did in the first two days, it was possible to contain the energy in the group, during a very difficult moment when E. Hopper came into the room. I imagine it would have had quite a destructive effect on a non-SCT group! Again, I was amazed at how we remained focused, supported each other in the subgroups, kept the energy inside the group and had some fun too.

Sixth member. One subgroup was exploring the impulse to stay in role and hold onto anger and not wanting to give up the role.

The door opened and an unfamiliar person came into the room. This person, who I thought was lost, walked over to the tea and biscuits and began to eat. He walked through into the other room and then quickly returned, pulling up a chair and continuing to eat. He stayed for the duration of the rest of the group occasionally swinging on his chair.

The leader told us she had forgotten to let the group know, or to ask the group, about the observer joining the group for the afternoon. Reactions that followed included shock, upset, disappointment, anger and some hysteria. The leader asked if we wanted to continue to work on roles and use this incident to continue to explore responses and reactions in subgroups. I felt outraged. Both with the observer and the leader. I felt cross, defiant, disempowered, childlike. The group had the work of integrating this new piece of information and new presence and re-establishing the boundaries. The group was, amazingly, gradually, slowly, able to explore and process the reactions and emotions, and I guess the retaliatory impulse, and continue the work of the group. This was made possible through subgrouping around experience and drawing attention back to the goals and making choices about how to continue working in the group. The member in the leadership training role and the group leader facilitated this process. Overall, the experience was hugely empowering and I learnt a great deal about the power of choice.

Discussion of the group and its trauma

From the SCT view: Susan

From the SCT view, the group's responses richly illustrated the phase dynamics that were stimulated, starting with authority, moving to the intimacy phase dynamics and lastly, recovering work phase functioning.

Authority. As with any living human system, the response to an unexpected break in structure and norms was inevitable: anger, outrage, paranoia, and dismissal of the authority were all part of the group's reactions. As one member said: "It seemed extraordinary that having an observer could be forgotten, and I don't think I really believed that this was what had happened. I felt really angry and assumed that Yvonne … had set this up". Another member recognized his care-taking impulse in response to the leader, but then focused on his own leadership behavior in the group, with little sense of Susan's leadership.

Intimacy. More important and more relevant for the purposes of this exposition, was that the break in structure and the failure of the leader to protect the group and extrude the intruder lessened the group's security. This precipitated the familiar personalized and stereotyped roles that groups use to organize in the face of anxiety and insecurity. This level of experience speaks to the underlying issues in the intimacy phase related to separation/individuation dynamics.

It is here that Earl's significant understanding of annihilation anxiety is most relevant. Earl apprehends the annihilation anxiety that is aroused in the intimacy conflicts, and elaborates an understanding of the oscillating role defenses that manage this level of experience. In this appreciation of the depth of the annihilation anxiety and the oscillation that manages it, (ba) I:A/M articulates a very important understanding of the underlying intimacy phase dynamics in living human systems that are invariably relevant in working with trauma.

At this level the basic role adaptations re-emerge and can be explored; role adaptations that manage survival and the experience of annihilation anxiety, the sense of falling apart (Agazarian, 1994). SCT works to develop the containment to explore the actual experience of "turned inside out" so that the experience can become more integrated and less encapsulated in survival roles.

Recovery to work. It was a testament to the group's overall development that they were able to continue working in cooperation with the leader's direction. Group members identified many of the pulls to old roles, with some recognition of how these roles helped them manage their personal responses, albeit stereotypically. The pull to the old roles signaled the degree of disruption in security as the group worked to re-establish its identity and security. Over time, the group returned to their membership roles, and subgrouped in the service of exploration and development, which enabled the group to re-establish a sense of structure and security. This was manifest in becoming more cohesive, using Hopper's (2003) three dimensions of cohesion, i.e., an increase in integration, solidarity and coherence, and, therefore, in the recovery of work group functioning.

Roles. Participants identified several possible roles, some of which were enacted, and others explored. Explicitly named were a defiant role, paranoid role, rescuer role, "rabbit in the headlights" role, show-off role, egoistic role, and targeting role ("them versus us"). Other roles can be inferred from the group's write-ups, e.g., a taking-charge role, the one-up role, an outraged role. Each of the role pulls would have a personal history for the members who felt or enacted them and simultaneously represent an attempt at group adaptation to the trauma precipitated by failed dependency.

For the group-as-a-whole, each role was a group adaptation, containing part of the group's reaction and attempting to remedy the break in security. Eventually, participants sought subgroup affiliations. Each of the subgroups also played a role in the group's work to stabilize and repair itself. The constellation of roles and subgroups then represented the group's adaptation to the traumatic event.

Many of the participants remembered an impulse to turn to the leader to manage and solve the problem of the intruder, only to discover that the leader had in fact introduced the problem. SCT would expect that when dependency has failed, the earlier role solutions with strong roots to the attachment system dynamics would manifest in an attempt to stabilize the group. In fact, several members reported their sense of the group banding together and supporting each other, as seen in their insistence that this trauma would have been destructive to a "non-SCT" group. This reflected the emergence of enchantment, or what Earl calls massification, in response to the annihilation anxiety associated with broken primal attachments, or what Earl calls aggregation. One member reported the impulse to disappear down the rabbit hole into herself and her body, and another member reported "being different" and that he did not introduce this as the basis for another functional subgroup (both responses being aspects of "withdrawing roles"). Both roles are related to avoidance or to what SCT terms the disenchantment roles in intimacy, in which the early role solutions related to premature separation, which is similar to Earl's assumption of aggregation. In effect, at the intimacy level in which the main issues are those of early attachment and separation/individuation, the group produced the two predictable, implicit subgroups, holding the complementary solutions: one subgroup holding the disenchantment roles of aggregation, and one holding the enchantment roles of what Earl calls massification.

Functional subgrouping for exploring the roles. Using functional subgrouping is especially important here to re-establish the group system to support the exploration of the response to the break in security. Stabilization through old roles is much more likely to promote survival at the expense of development. In contrast, stabilizing with functional subgrouping increases the potential for both survival and development, and ultimately transformation. Linking to the theory of incohesion, functional subgrouping provides a secure containment for exploring the annihilation anxiety (through discriminating and integrating the experience) that the role encapsulations and oscillations manage. Thus, with functional subgrouping, the oscillations can be organized in the service of development instead of defense and fixation.

Needless to say, the "surprise" observer was challenging to the leader as well as to the group. Mostly, I managed this by holding the SCT structure and norms for exploring. This enabled a "good enough" group containment for the group to explore the responses to the break in structure and norms. Yet, in retrospect, there was additional work that would have been useful. The role solutions that the group was holding might have been reframed in a way that enabled the group to explore the two kinds of intimacy roles that the group was naming in two functional subgroups, i.e., exploring the enchantment roles in one subgroup, and then in turn, the disenchantment roles in the other subgroup. This would have maximized the opportunity for repair to the group-as-a-whole and, isomorphically, repair in each member. Or put in terms of Earl's theory of incohesion, functional subgrouping could be used to contain the intra-psychic or intra-personal oscillation from crustacean to amoeboid, and the inter-psychic or inter-personal oscillation between aggregation and massification, until the information contained in the two sides of the oscillation could be explored and integrated, first in the security of functional subgrouping, and then in the group-as-a-whole.

Thus, from an SCT perspective, this group trauma from failed dependency provoked roles with roots in basic attachment styles related to the intimacy dynamics and separation/individuation issues. An understanding of the annihilation anxiety managed by these roles is in fact enormously useful in deepening this SCT leader's understanding of the intimacy phase challenges.

From the group analytical and psychological view: Earl

This event and the processes that followed from it can be understood in terms of my theory of the fourth basic assumption in the unconscious "life" of groups, which I have termed Incohesion: Aggregation/Massification or, in the time honoured tradition of basic assumption theory, (ba) I:A/M. Of course, in terms of classical psychoanalytical theory the traumatising event that precipitated the authority phase was associated with unconscious Oedipal dynamics. I was experienced as a paternal, sexual, phallic intruder into the individual children of the "mother" group and its "maternal leader", and into the "mind" of the group and into the mind of its "maternal leader". Mother turned a blind eye, and neglected to protect her children from this intrusion. The children were also exposed to a primal scene experience in which they had to cope with their sudden awareness that their leaders, Susan and Yvonne, had relationships with Earl that allowed this to have been arranged "behind the scenes", so to say.

In terms of my theory of (ba) I:A/M, the traumatising event must also be conceptualized in terms of the dynamics of profound helplessness. Moreover, the empirical material illustrates, in order: intrusion and broken boundaries, failed dependency, the fear of annihilation and its vicissitudes involving psychic fission and fragmentation oscillating with psychic fusion and confusion, the development of crustacean and/or amoeboid personality structures, intra-psychic encapsulations, aggregation oscillating with massification, the development of roles associated with aggregation and massification, role suction, personifications of roles by people who have developed crustacean and/or amoeboid personality organization, particular patterns of aggressive feelings and scapegoating, and the development of enclaves and ghettos.

Personification of aggregation was seen first in crustacean/lone wolf functioning, for example, in one member's reflection: "I became much more self-conscious, started to lose a systems perspective, went into my head, and became somewhat alienated from the group". The personification of massification was then seen in amoeboid/morale boosting functioning, for example, in another member's singing the praises of SCT and the skills that it provided. However, the projection of extreme incompetence onto me as the observer, who was defined as being outside the SCT framework, was essential to the development and maintenance of the massification process. I broke SCT rules about how to conduct an observation, and, therefore, was, to say the least, unwelcome, especially because I interrupted illusions of massification or what SCT terms "enchantment". In fact, I was scapegoated, which was essential for the development and maintenance of the massification process. It is important to take note of how the group perceived the scapegoat in terms of his relationships to the leader of the group, and how he was used by the group to protect the leader from their own aggression towards her. Clearly the group worked very hard to recover their work group functioning, which they did achieve by the end of the session. Nonetheless, this recovery was associated with massification processes. In the same way that all basic assumptions can be functional for particular kinds of work group activity (e.g., during times of war, the fight/flight basic assumption serves work group processes that are required by the military and by a citizenry mobilized for war), massification serves the development and maintenance of morale. However, it is essential to move beyond massification as a form of inauthentic cohesion, to shift from morale boosting to more genuine group charisma.

This empirical material illustrates how important it is to focus on unconscious meanings of communications. Without wishing to be self-protective, I would suggest that in reality I was not all *that* horrible, and Susan and Yvonne, all *that* marvelous. For example, why was Susan and Yvonne's "oversight" "forgotten" so quickly? I would suggest that the group's experience of it was encapsulated, and the group-as-a-whole began to develop into a kind of cult, enclave or ghetto against the outside world of the mental health professions and of alternative systems and styles of organizational consultation. It would be well worth considering what my counter-transference might tell us about what I was witnessing and what might have been projected into me, but this is beyond the scope of the present paper.

Concluding discussion

Susan. In summary, Earl's understanding of the oscillating role defenses that manage the annihilation anxiety is extremely useful for SCT. In the intimacy phase work that is so essential in working with trauma, SCT emphasizes containing the pull to the role oscillation in functional subgrouping. As each set of roles is contained and then explored in turn, the information encapsulated by the role and related to the annihilation anxiety therein can be discriminated and integrated, thereby potentiating system development rather than the fixation of oscillation (Agazarian, 2003).

SCT emphasizes system dynamics, while basic assumption theory emphasizes the psychodynamics, or to put this another way, SCT begins with the dynamics of the most comprehensive system and its subsystems, and basic assumption theory begins with the psychodynamics of the members of the system. Of course, Earl's version of basic assumption theory conceptualizes persons as members of the system, and SCT fully recognizes that members of systems have psychodynamics. Yet, rather than focusing on psychodynamics, SCT conceptualizes system dynamics as isomorphic at all levels of a system, including the person. SCT focuses on building the system that can explore whatever dynamics emerge, so the information/energy can be discriminated and integrated in the service of system development at all system levels.

In a book review of Hopper's (2003) book, written a year before this group event occurred, Agazarian (2003, p. 4) compared the two approaches:

> ... Hopper's Theory of Incohesion complements our [SCT] thinking ... (by offering) ... a deeper understanding of the dynamics of the phase of intimacy. (However) ... we explain the splitting that occurs in the Intimacy Phase in terms of the vicissitudes of discrimination and integration in the process of separation and individuation: attributing separation to discriminating differences in the apparently similar and individuation to discriminating similarities in the apparently different. The deeper, psychodynamic experiences of alienation we explain in terms of a barrier experience in which there is a primary split between good and bad which makes it impossible to discriminate the good in the bad or the bad in the good. Thus the emergence of the roles characterized either by alienation and blind despair or by merging and blind hope. Where Hopper is importantly different in his approach is that both his thinking and his interpretation of group and individual dynamics are deeply related to the personal and social unconscious, whereas ours are related to the development of apprehensive containment that enables the individual and the group to discover titrated layers of unconscious material.

In this context it seems relevant to take note of one other difference. At the personal level, in writing this paper, I have found myself wanting to protect the group from pathologizing interpretations of their responses to this traumatic event, especially in so far as such pathologizing interpretations may be experienced as another intrusive traumatic event. Yet I do not think my impulse is purely personal in that it is here that the differences in the emphasis on psychodynamics and system dynamics are most pronounced. Though a detailed exploration of the differences is beyond the scope of this paper, it is perhaps most relevant to note these differences in terms of working with trauma. From a systems perspective, framing human dynamics in terms of psychopathology risks increasing the personalization of the group responses in a way that closes the boundaries to exploration rather than opens them. Looking at a system solution in context detoxifies the understanding of both the group solutions and the personalized solutions, and creates a system for exploration that enhances the potential for development. More importantly, the similarities in our understandings still stand out even as we differ in our methods.

Earl. This material illustrates how the basic assumption of Inco-hesion is more relevant to the understanding of the fear of annihila-tion than it is to Oedipal anxieties, although these anxieties are often interrelated. Failed dependency is not only a matter of an incestuous event coupled with the sense that mother has turned a blind eye, but also a matter of the more general experience of profound helpless-ness and fear of annihilation that follow from actual damage, aban-donment and loss, which are the main ingredients of a traumatogenic process which involves ruptures in the safety shield. Thus, the merg-ers of massification are not about removing the father as much as they are about becoming part of all that is maternal, although this is obviously a matter of emphasis. The responses by the commu-nity and significant others to the traumatized are very important in determining the severity of both short and longer-term sequelae of traumatic experience. Susan's behavior, and, in turn, the behavior of most of the individuals in the group, facilitated their returning to work group functioning. Their behavior reflected the skills that they had developed in the context of SCT. However, I believe that I would have achieved the same outcomes, but on the basis of clari-fication, holding, containing and ultimately interpretation of the unconscious aspects of traumatic experience. I hope that within a therapy or a training group these experiences would be metabolized in a way that enabled the participants in the group to feel, think and behave in more "mature" ways, not only in the group but also in other contexts.

I take issue with Susan's belief that basic assumption theory and interventions based on it serve to "pathologize" a particular set of group dynamics and its personification by particular individuals, unless she believes that anxiety and burdensome defenses against it mean "pathology". There can hardly be any doubt that under cer-tain circumstances people experience Oedipal anxieties and psy-chotic anxieties. Moreover, some people experience such anxieties more intensely and more regularly than do others, and do so at inappropriate times and places. Help with these anxieties is available through well-timed and empathic transference interpretations. After all, to what does "trauma" refer, if not to "pathology?" And to whom does SCT offer "therapy", if not to people who say that they need help with their suffering and problems? Nonetheless, I do not think of groups or systems in terms of pathology and the pathological. When I work as a consultant to organizations to which I refer metaphorically as "traumatized", "wounded", or "broken", and less metaphorically as "disrupted", I find that anxiety is rife among their personnel. These anxieties can be traced to various characteristics of the organizational systems. Thus, I think of these organizations as "pathogenic", in that they have become structured in ways that cause their personnel to feel anxious. Such anxiety is a natural, normal and healthy response to danger.

I often work in organizations and in countries in which high levels of anxiety are statistically normal. Thus, so too, is (ba) I:A/M. This basic assumption is functional in that it seems to be necessary for psychic survival. Without (ba) I:A/M groups might fall apart much more quickly and totally than they so often do (which is also the case with respect to the other three basic assumptions of dependency, fight/flight and pairing).

One of the ways in which my approach differs from that of SCT and Yvonne's theory is that whereas SCT assumes isomorphism among all "levels" of living human systems in a defined hierarchy, I take isomorphism as problematic. Moreover, personification and valence in association with role suction refer to the problematic interface between the dynamics of personal systems and the dynamics of social systems. The nature of this problematic interface cannot and should not be assumed. More importantly, this degree of isomorphism contains vital information, an exploration of which can be used in the service of psychotherapy as well as consultation to the organization. In part, this is a matter of the "location" of a particular event or communication in a particular system. However, location must also be understood in terms of perception and frame of reference, rather than "level", which are or should be, a matter for negotiation between the observer and the observed.

In conclusion

A strong emphasis on theory guides practice, and the exploration of differences in theory and in practice contribute to the development of both. We hope that this chapter illustrates our commitment to this point of view. We are not afraid of trying together to elucidate the similarities and differences in our work and how we think about it. To the contrary. We welcome the exploration of our respective points of view. Writing the articles on which this chapter is based has brought us closer, and enhanced our commitment to working in and with living human systems.

References

Agazarian, Y. M. (1994). The phases of development and the systems-centered group. In Pines, M. & Schermer, V. (Eds.), *Ring of fire: Primitive object relations and affect in group psychotherapy*. London: Routledge, Chapman & Hall.

Agazarian, Y. M. (1997). *Systems-centered therapy for groups*. New York: Guilford Press. Re-printed in paperback (2004). London: Karnac Books.

Agazarian, Y. M. (2003). Book review. [Review of the book *Traumatic experience in the unconscious life of groups*, by Hopper, E.]. In *Systems-Centered Training News*, 11(1), 3–4.

Gantt, S. P. & Hopper, E. (2008a). Two perspectives on a trauma in a training group: The systems-centered approach and the theory of incohesion (part I). *Group Analysis*, 41(1), 98–112. doi: 10.1177/0533316408088416.

Gantt, S. P. & Hopper, E. (2008b). Two perspectives on a trauma in a training group: The systems-centered approach and the theory of incohesion (part II). *Group Analysis*, 41(2), 123–139. doi: 10.1177/0533316408089879.

Hopper, E. (2003). *Traumatic experience in the unconscious life of groups*. London: Jessica Kingsley Publishers.

CHAPTER FOUR

Role, goal and context: key issues for group therapists and group leaders

Christer Sandahl, Ph.D.

Yvonne Agazarian has been a teacher and a friend ever since she explained the System for Analysing Verbal Interaction (SAVI) to me by scribbling on a table napkin at a dinner party twenty years ago. She has inspired and helped me to develop my skills as a group conductor and a leader of different groups. As a group analytic psychotherapist, it has been a challenge to integrate systems-centered training (SCT) into the work, partly due to difficulties that can arise in relation to the social context of theories such as group analysis or SCT. Some people get suspicious and feel that one is abandoning their preferred theoretical assumptions if one starts to integrate new ideas into one's thinking and actual practising of the profession. It is not a problem with the theories per se, because they do need to be developed, but it is a challenge with respect to one's personal need of belongingness. That is a price I believe you have to pay in order to maintain your freedom and not become corrupted by the theories in the sense that critical thinking is lost. During our careers, we encounter only a few persons who can be helpful in this tricky balancing act, and who become important for our own thinking and professional practice. Yvonne is definitely one of those people, and, in particular, she is one who will not let you sit and contemplate your ideas and preconceptions alone in peace and quiet.

Another such person was Bruce Reed, the founder of the Grubb Institute for Behavioural Studies in London. Under no circumstances did he ever stop asking me challenging questions! As far as I know, Yvonne never met Bruce before he died in 2003. Nonetheless, many of their ideas about systems thinking and its integration with psychoanalysis are very similar, especially regarding the importance of understanding how to adopt a role as a leader or therapist. I have also personally experienced their compassion and care, which has led me to look upon them as my professional parents. This might seem strange considering the fact that they never met, but perhaps we can let them come together here? How can a leader of groups understand the aspects of *role*, *goal*, and *context*, if different perspectives are allowed to influence and reshape each other? In order to explain this, I need to start by describing how leadership can be comprehended. My aim is to illustrate the similarities between the role of manager and the role of group psychotherapist.

Leadership

Being a manager entails continuous exposure to emotionally challenging situations. For example, simply having to chair a meeting can be a strenuous event. Something unexpected can suddenly occur; a sensitive issue can arise that the manager is not prepared for. One person can launch a personal attack on someone else, and others can have planned to pose a question involving serious criticism of the chair as a manager. Or consider this classic situation: a meeting is sluggish and quiet, but when it is over everyone engages in lively conversation as they are leaving, while the chairperson has no idea what is going on. All managers are required to perform tasks that can include challenges that put their judgement, social competence, or motivation to the test. As managers, they can easily end up in situations that they feel they cannot handle very well, or criticism voiced by others can make them painfully aware that that may indeed be the case.

With this as a background, it becomes apparent that leadership involves more feelings and relationships than most managers generally imagine. Considering this aspect, there are several similarities between the role of being manager and the role of being a group psychotherapist. These disparate roles obviously have completely different objectives, but the processes and dynamics in the relationships that are dealt with in the work can be similar. The fact that the tasks to be performed per se include interpersonal relationships, conflicts, authority problems, and communication makes the work complicated and emotionally challenging. To a large extent, a professional with the role of either manager or psychotherapist is required to use him- or herself as a tool.

In other words, being able to accept and adopt a role as manager or group leader in a responsible way requires psychological work that is sometimes underestimated. From this perspective, group psychotherapists often have an advantage, since most training programs in this area take into account the complexity of the role. Trust, clarity, and consideration constitute the basis of good leadership of any type of group. For managers, this involves taking care of staff members as well as the operations of and people targeted by the organisation. Managers are also expected to solve problems that can arise at any time, such as the need to settle conflicts in work teams or in relations with other actors within or outside of the organisation. In simple terms, it is necessary to wield authority, and most managers find it difficult to do so in a respectful and non-authoritarian manner. For instance, it is pointless to tell someone that "From now on, I am your authority!" since that person might not care less. In contrast to exercising power, having authority involves being given the right to sanction or authorise. Authority emanates from the trust and confidence of others, and it presupposes that those who are affected can agree upon the goal of the operations, and that they are aware of what needs to be done. Under such circumstances, everyone has the potential to act with authority, regardless of whether they are managers or not. Acting with authority involves taking initiatives and working to reach the common overall goal of the organisation. Leadership built on authority, in contrast to that based on wielding power, creates trust and meaning, both in the organisation and in society in general (Reed & Bazalgette, 2006). Unlike most other forms of psychotherapy, in SCT it is very clear that the leader of a group must use his or her authority, especially when the group is in the early stages of development. (See Agazarian, 1997, pp. 84–86 for the SCT view around leader/therapist role in "Defense Modification in the Phases of Group Development".) There are marked similarities in the way that leadership is exercised in SCT and in an ordinary work team.

The core of leadership of therapy groups and work teams is about knowing oneself and dealing with the emotions that arise from the work and from insight into the vulnerability, the dependence, and the responsibility that are elements of the role (Badaracco, 2006). In that way, leadership is more of an art than a science. It is a matter of knowing who you are and, to the best of your ability, understanding your motives and using your empathy and intuition to act at the right moment; that is, you have to realise whether you should act now or bide your time, or if you should avoid a particular action (Badaracco, 2002). In general, the idea of experiencing oneself as a person also involves experiencing other people, compassion, comprehension, and participation. A person is like a node in a network of communication and dependence. To describe this, Foulkes (1964) has used the term "matrix", which also has the connotation of uterus or mould. As a person, I can represent other people, realise how I affect them, and admit to myself how I am influenced by them. Accordingly, work is about achieving something together with other people, something that is significant in its social and historical context.

The Danish theologian and philosopher Løgstrup (1997) stated this in a similar manner, when he described how dependent we are on the way that other people respond to our actions, indicating that there is an intrinsic ethical demand in all relationships. Løgstrup said that we place our lives in the hands of others. He meant that we have a responsibility for each other that goes beyond what is most evident, namely, we are accountable for how what we say and do might be perceived by other people on a personal level. Notwithstanding, we can never know how our actions and words will be apprehended and interpreted by those around us. In other words, Løgstrup implied that we require dialogue to be able to live up to the ethical demand. There is considerable ethical responsibility associated with the leader's role (in therapy groups and work teams), and the power of the impact of someone assuming authority should not be underestimated. Nonetheless, it is also a moral responsibility to take on authority, if it is apparent that such action is needed. In any case, it is important to be sensitive and conscientious.

Needless to say, there is a rhythm in human interactions to which we should train our sensitivity. This is related to emotions and also to intellectual acumen and discipline—*both* feelings *and* common sense. It is a question of *putting the goal of the organisation ahead of your own immediate needs and impulses, without losing contact with the emotions you are experiencing at that particular moment* (Sandahl, et al., 2010).

Being able to refrain from immediately displaying emotions is part of being a professional group leader. This does not mean that a manager should never show feelings; just the opposite, because the leader would otherwise be regarded as callous. However, a person who is a manager or a psychotherapist needs to be in contact with his/her emotions but must also be able to decide when feelings should be suppressed and when showing them openly will serve the purpose at hand.

Context

The way that leadership is conducted is determined not only by the personality and experience of the individual in question, but certainly also by the requirements stipulated by the organisation in the form of aspects such as culture, rules, rights, and resources. For example, a cynical and harsh frame of mind among top management will spread to subordinates in different ways, and the same type of dissemination will occur in the opposite situation in which the most superior managers have high integrity and treat each other with respect. Individual managers or treatment providers will be affected by all these work environment factors, which also place limitations on what can or cannot be done. In addition, a manager's closest co-workers, or the members of a therapy group, will play a decisive role, not the least because of the way they interpret the actions of their superior and the extent to which they can and are willing to take responsibility for or lead some aspects of the work that is to be done. Moreover, there can be subgroups that for various reasons feel they have the right to undermine the leader's authority, or, in the opposite case, there can be responsible and independent people who think it is their duty to make the utmost effort to achieve the common goals. Both those situations will have a marked impact on the person who is in charge.

In this view, leadership is not vested in individuals, but rather might be regarded as a function of several factors: the leader as a person, the organisation and the context that people belong to, and the group members' relationship with the organisation as a whole and with the manager. This way of explaining leadership is illustrated in the following figure:

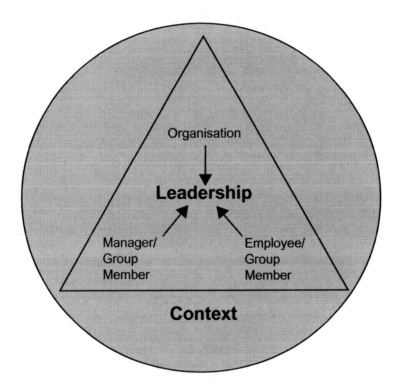

In other words, as a leader, a person is dependent on the members of the group as well as the organisation as a whole and its stipulations, not least considering how this is manifested among the top leaders and the immediate manager. However, this dependence is mutual. The leader's way of acting will, in turn, affect the work environment and culture. These things do not occur solely on a conscious and rational level.

In organisational psychology, two concepts have been developed to distinguish between the conscious (preconscious) and the unconscious internal image or picture of the organisation (Hutton-Reed, 2000).

- *Institution*, which is a social entity that has been created for a specific function that is official or unofficial, or formal or informal, in nature, for example a family, a business, a church, a government, or a voluntary organisation.
- *Organisation*, which describes how "the institution" is structured and arranged so that human and material resources can be used to achieve the overall aim.

The organisation in the mind concerns our inner images and feelings related to roles, aims, rituals, responsibility, competence, failures, and successes. On the other hand, *the institution in the mind* comprises the unconscious existentially charged notions and emotions that are linked to the organisation with respect to factors such as values, dogmas, expectations, ideals, birth, life, and death. *The organisation within us* can be perceived as a metaphor for the body, and *the institution within us* can represent a metaphor for the spark of life or the spirit. Together they form a whole.

Thus the emotional experience influences work relationships on both a conscious level (*the organisation within us*) and a subconscious level (*the institution within us*). As a leader or co-worker, I want to be rooted in reality, but reality obviously consists of so much more than can actually be observed. To be realistic, I need to understand how I consciously and unconsciously deal with the strains of work. The more I comprehend about my inner world, the better I can handle reality. The "soft" values such as emotions contain important information not only about myself and the way I am, but also about the condition of the organisation as a whole.

All the people employed at a hospital or a bank can obviously agree on what organisation it is they work in, but, if they were asked to describe their organisation, they would give very different accounts of the particular hospital or bank. Their "inner pictures" of their organisations differ because they are not created solely by the formal organisation plan or any documented criteria for evaluation or officially adopted ethical codes. Such inner images are created by each individual's unique and emotionally significant experiences of and exposure to organisations. They are the results of what experiences we have had with regard to formal and informal roles, functions, relationships, or cooperation and power.

In particular as a superior, a person can tend to expect that all staff members will share his/her own image of the organisation and its objectives, which are often very explicit and obviously close at hand for the manager. However, that is not always the case and may indeed even be a rare event. This is one of the most trying aspects that face managers, some of whom can even consider the situation to be desperate, which can be expressed as follows: "I've talked at the meetings, I've written memos, I've sent emails, I've asked others to talk on the subject. How much information do I have to provide to make them understand? It's hopeless". Nevertheless, the problem in these cases is not related to a lack of information, but rather to a lack of time for open discussion and exchange of ideas.

This is not merely a matter of unconscious feelings and processes. If we just stop and think about it, we ourselves are fairly well aware of our inner picture of the organisation. However, we are seldom conscious of the factors that have created it, which invariably emanate from our life experiences. On the contrary, we often forget that it is our own personal image that we need to communicate to others and we need to take into consideration, the latter requirement being especially important for a leader. What are your views on the organisation? How would you describe it? In your opinion, what is its objective? Only if this is done, will it be possible to share our different images and arrive at common pictures. This dialogue is also a necessary part of group psychotherapy. A key aspect of therapeutic alliance in group psychotherapy is that the members share an idea about the overall purpose of the therapy, and that they have a similar understanding about how the group is supposed to work.

However, for a therapist, it may be most important to pose this type of question to him- or herself. As a treatment provider, are my opinions about the organisation and why we exist the same as those held by the people who lead the work, or am I carrying on some kind of subversive activity under the pretext that it is best for the patients? If the latter is true, it would be important to clarify and scrutinize my motives both to myself and my colleagues, and I would need to be able to explain how my actions are conducive to the overall purpose of the organisation.

The purpose of the organisation is the ultimate "compass bearing" that determines whether a person can perform professionally as a manager or co-worker. If the purpose is obscure, or if there is no purpose, which is not uncommon, it is impossible to be professional in one's role. Without a purpose, there is no system in which to have a role. Under such conditions, ambitious staff or managers usually attempt to proceed by trial and error. As long as possible, they try to define the purpose as they assume it to be. This search for the purpose and meaning of the operations can result in growing feelings of confusion, as the sense of direction and context is lost. It becomes necessary for individuals to rely on themselves and other people, which gives free rein to cliques and conflicts. Also, it becomes extremely difficult to understand why certain people succeed and are rewarded and given positions in the organisation, while others are ignored or are regarded as troublesome. What is guiding the operations in the workplace? It is impossible to answer that question. If the situation continues and an individual and his/her colleagues are not given the opportunity to formulate and become familiar with a shared purpose, there is a substantial risk that, in an effort to be professional, the person will instead become drained and burned out, and will be looked upon as inconvenient or bothersome and sometimes become the scapegoat. In SCT such processes are usually prevented, but it can frequently be observed in other forms of group therapy that the patients are confused about purpose and working methods.

Purpose is often confused with goal. Most organisations have some form of goal, but that does not mean that they also have a purpose. A goal is usually described as something that is concrete and attainable, and can be monitored and measured. A purpose gives meaning to the goal. The purpose is the ultimate intention of the goal, its aim: Why do we actually do what we do? A well-conceived purpose is more important than the individual organisation. It appeals to our inner passions, to our basic values and beliefs. It answers the question of what the operations of the organisation aim to achieve—*why* we do what we do.

Role

The term "role" often appears in social psychology, and it is frequently defined as being equivalent to the expectations that are placed on a person. In an occupational context, role is sometimes regarded as being comparable to a work description: "Your role is to ... " The limitation of such definitions is that they are directive and static; someone else is defining our roles. However, that is hardly the way it works in practice. No one can do a job merely by following work instructions, and problems soon arise if we simply do what others expect us to do. In all occupations, it eventually becomes necessary to make independent judgments and prioritisations. Moreover, it must be taken into account how the choices that can be made are affected by dynamic and variable surroundings.

Another way to consider role is illustrated by group psychology, in which it is common to designate roles such as these: the talkative one, the informal leader, the quiet one, and the person in need, etcetera. Furthermore, a deep psychological (Jungian) version of organisational psychology has given role names such as the following: the king, the princess, the hero, the wise woman, the witch, and the clown, etcetera. The fundamental concept is that, under the surface in each group or organisation, a drama is unfolding that comprises an array of roles, and the way that people act is influenced by factors such as history, context, task, and group composition. Indeed, it can be rather amusing and interesting to use fairy tales to try to identify the roles that different people have adopted in your own workplace.

We often take different roles in different contexts. A person who is very reserved and quiet at work can be happy and talkative outside the workplace, and may even be the one who makes all the decisions at home. Is it possible for us to act in opposite ways in different places and still be ourselves? Certainly, our personalities provide many options. Depending on the circumstances, we can display disparate facets of ourselves and still express the same fundamental and indivisible identity. Successful actors know that, to be convincing on stage, they have to discover something within themselves that is in harmony with the characters they are supposed to portray and the issues that are to be created in a play. The same thing applies to clowns; to simply act like a buffoon will frighten children instead of entertaining them and making them happy.

The problem with applying stereotype roles such as *the quiet one, the provoker, the princess, the clown,* and *the know-it-all* is that the individual in question is to some extent a victim of the circumstances and even his/her own unconscious. Roles of this type often serve to inhibit the development and maturation of both the individual and the group to which he/she belongs. The more you learn to know yourself, and the more you understand what psychological roles you have a propensity for and that the group would prefer that you select, the more you can make your own choice. Do I really want to play this role again? Do I have any other prospects that I want to take advantage of and that can better serve our group and our purpose?

SCT has another way of defining role (see Agazarian, 1997, pp. 70–71 for an SCT introduction of role) that starts from the above discussion concerning organisations as both external reality and internal representations. It means that role can be perceived as a function of both the organisation per se and who the individual is as a person. Using that perspective, the role is placed on the actor and not on the surroundings. This means that the adoption of a role can be regarded as a regulating principle that exists within a person (Reed & Bazalgette, 2006).

The role becomes a way to guide behaviours in relation to what needs to be done to achieve the overall purpose. For example, in a family with children, one intention is probably to ensure that the children will eventually become young adults who are able to leave the family and start their own complete and rewarding lives. A family obviously has other purposes as well, but the roles as mother and father have their starting point in the mentioned intention. Furthermore, a role is continually changing. Children grow up, and things are always happening both within and outside the family that must be taken into consideration. Being the father of a five-year-old is quite different from being the father of a seven-year-old. When a parent has to relinquish a certain way of acting that is associated with a particular way of perceiving an offspring, it can lead to feelings of frustration and sadness—or for that matter, also relief and contentment—but it will always be connected with some kind of emotion, at least if the parent cares about the child.

A role is dynamic and must be constantly altered and adjusted to fit the existing circumstances, even though the purpose remains unchanged. It is analogous to sailing: you cannot simply take a compass bearing and steer towards a destination, but rather you must continuously take into account and exploit the winds to your advantage. At times it can seem that the direction you have chosen is completely wrong, but, under the prevailing conditions, it may be the only way to reach the goal of the journey. The same thing applies to a group, because adopting a role is an endless and dynamic task in which various factors must be taken into consideration. For the leader of a group, as for the skipper of a boat or a parent, this process must be kept in focus at all times.

In working life, the professional role can be regarded as the difference between what is our private self and what becomes our professional self (i.e., how we handle ourselves at work). Bruce Reed developed a model of role that involves a balance between three different perspectives: (1) we ourselves as persons with our driving forces and desires; (2) the system in which we work and its purpose; (3) the context including the resources we have at our disposal. (This model is almost identical with the SCT approach, but the models have interestingly developed independently. See Agazarian, 1997, p. 32 for a starting point of the SCT view.) The task of adopting a role requires both time and energy, but it also generates energy and pleasure in work. One way of working towards "taking a role" has been developed at the Grubb Institute and is called Organisational Role Analysis (ORA).

The ORA process comprises the three steps of finding, forming, and lastly adopting a role. *Finding* your inner role entails discovering a place from which to act. It may be necessary to ask yourself what the main task actually is. What does the organisation look like if you delve behind formal structures? What power groups and actors are in the arena, and what resources are available? It can be necessary to consider the surroundings that you act in socially, religiously, and culturally. Finally, you need to ask yourself what aspects of your experience, knowledge, and abilities are adequate in the situation at hand.

The use of such questions can make it possible to discover whether there is a role that fits. In the subsequent phase, it is necessary to clarify your feelings and thoughts about *how the role can be formed* (or "made"). You need to decide whether you feel committed to the operations of the organisation and preferably also on what grounds (to be able to take on responsibility). It is difficult to assume a role in an organisation if you are not interested in its objective. (In the long run, working solely to earn a living and have as much leisure time as possible leads to alienation and the risk of burnout, and you can no longer make useful contributions to the organisation.) It is necessary to find out whether your own picture of the organisation agrees with what others think. How realistic is the actual description of the situation? Perhaps you have had experiences that limit your understanding in that context. It is not a matter of cold analysis, but rather a process that involves the whole person.

This work creates a belief in personal strength and abilities. In some cases it entails explaining to yourself and others what you plan to do to benefit the system, so that the organisation can achieve its purpose and goal. This is very different from accomplishing your own personal goals. By taking the risk that is associated with influencing other people, you use your authority, which in turn generally makes it easier for others to show their authority.

By *taking a role* in this way, a person can contribute to a culture that is based on freedom and personal responsibility rather than control. In as much as the world around us is constantly changing, it is not possible to arrive at a conclusive method of developing and adopting a role. In the role of manager or group conductor, it is necessary to act like the skipper of a boat, who must always be aware of what is happening in and outside the vessel, and in the direction of travel in both the short and the long term. After assuming a role in this manner, it may become evident that the purpose has to be altered. In that case, part of the role involves use of authority to allow the individual to act in a fashion that will facilitate and contribute to the desired change.

To take the role in such a dynamic fashion gives a lot of freedom. One can relate to persons within the system in a personal *and* professional way at the same time. One does not have to hide behind organisational or hierarchical structures, but can act with responsibility, empathy and ethical sensitivity. Neither is one restricted to a single role. In other situations, in the context of other systems with other purposes, one can use and demonstrate other parts of oneself, sometimes with the same people as one encountered in another role. There can be a pleasure to be in a new role, and surprise people by revealing parts of oneself, which might be for them unknown personal talents or gifts.

References

Agazarian, Y. M. (1997). *Systems-centered therapy for groups*. New York: Guilford Press. Re-printed in paperback (2004). London: Karnac Books.

Badaracco, J. L. (2002). *Leading quietly: An unorthodox guide to doing the right thing*. Boston: Harvard Business School Press.

Badaracco, J. L. (2006). *Questions of character: Illuminating the heart of leadership through literature*. Boston: Harvard Business School Press.

Foulkes, S. H. (1964). *Therapeutic group analysis*. London: Karnac Books.

Hutton-Reed, J. M. (2000). *Working with the concept of the organisation-in-the-mind*. London: The Grubb Institute.

Løgstrup, K. (1997). *The ethical demand*. Notre Dame: The University of Notre Dame Press.

Reed, B. & Bazalgette, J. (2006). Organisational role analysis at the Grubb Institute of Behavioural Studies: Origins and development. In Newton, J. (Ed.), *Coaching in depth. The organisational role analysis approach*. London: Karnac Books.

Sandahl, C., Falkenström, E. & von Knorring, M. (2010). *Chef med känsla och förnuft. Om professionalism och etik i ledarskapet (Manager with feelings and common sense. About professional and ethical leadership)*. Stockholm: Natur & Kultur.

CHAPTER FIVE

SCT and psychodynamic group psychotherapy

Walter N. Stone, M.D., CGP, DFAGPA

Abstract

This paper explores the applications of Systems-Centered therapy (SCT) to Psychodynamic therapy (PD). Both theories are based on analytic principles, but achieve their results through differing interventions. Functional subgrouping is unique to SCT, and it is the major method for discriminating and integrating differences and developing a systems-centered group. Important commonalities include a focus on the here-and-now of the meeting, members' immediate experience, and the emphasis on group dynamics that highlight members' roles in representing and working for the group. Both systems appreciate that groups gradually develop and mature and members become more able to use the concepts, including the "jargon" of the system to advance the work of the group.

Examples from demonstration groups and from clinical experiences are used to illustrate the different types of interventions made by clinicians from the two theoretical perspectives. The paper ends with the author's reflections on the evolution and development of SCT therapy over more than thirty years of observation.

Introduction

Choosing a title for this paper has been a challenge, because a title often reflects the author's point of view about the topic. Thus I had to find the word or phrase that most accurately reflected my view of the value of integrating aspects of SCT into more traditional psychodynamic group treatment. Before choosing the more narrow title using "application", I explored several other words, checking this out with my Webster's New Collegiate Dictionary.

This process actually helped clarify my thinking about the relevance of the SCT model. Relevance: "relation to the matter at hand: practical and especially social applicability". Using the term "relevance" seemed too general and did not capture the essence of my understanding of the value of SCT formulations. I then toyed with "overlapping", which seemed closer, in that it conveyed two theories having commonalities but also distinctive elements. However, such an understanding does not then emphasize the particular manner in which SCT emphasized ways of thinking about, and responding to, commonly observable phenomenon. Confluence was a word that might describe my perspective. Referring to Webster, confluence is: "a coming or flowing together, meeting or gathering at one point". The theories are based upon psychoanalytic principles, but they do not come together, rather I see them perhaps starting together, and then flowing in divergent, but parallel paths. The first example is used to illustrate the differing roles of the therapist, as they strive to help members learn to focus on the emotions evoked in the immediacy of the group interaction.

Clinical Illustrations

Example

Training for group therapists often includes volunteering to participate in a demonstration group in order for an instructor to illustrate aspects of a theory or of leadership. In one such experience a married couple volunteered. Their marital status was unknown to the leader and to several of the individuals who volunteered to be "members".

After a modest period of time, a sudden conflict arose in which the wife rather angrily commented to her husband that he was responding to her just as he did at home: he was not paying attention and not responding to her. He clearly was embarrassed by this confrontation.

The SCT therapist would note that the participants were not in a member role, but in a "person system". They would also be in the past rather than present time frame. He might ask them to speak from these two perspectives. The therapist might also ask who was feeling angry at the moment (not specifically angry at the couple) and form subgroups of persons who felt angry and those who did not. This "generalization" of anger would be designed to avoid scapegoating the couple for causing "trouble" or discomfort in the group. Similarly, SCT might ask what the couple was containing for the group that was being put in the outside role relationship rather than explored by the group.

The psychodynamic (PD) group therapist is also faced with a number of choices. He has to deal with his own and others' surprise and affect in response to the member's announcement. He would have to take into account that a portion of the membership knew of the relationship and others did not. One intervention might simply be to comment that it is somewhat startling to see a marital conflict emerge in the group, and wonder what people are experiencing. This addresses the immediate affect within the group. If the opportunity arose, the therapist might wonder if members, who were aware of the presence of a married couple, might have had some inner responses to their presence. This would lead naturally to exploring the emotions of the others who had not known of the marriage.

Both SCT and PD clinicians focus on members' immediate affect in the here-and-now of the meeting. The SCT clinician by referring to the "person-system" might add that the individual is doing work for the group. This would be an explicit comment that includes the entire system. However, any intervention that appears to address a single individual is heard by everyone, which reinforces the norm of working in the present and as part of the whole group.

I have chosen this illustration to highlight the role of the therapist. The SCT therapist, particularly in the early phases of the group, trains group (confronting) members to discriminate their person system and to learn to bring their person into their member role. The request to form subgroups maintains a focus on the emotion and engages the entire group. The PD therapist's approach also focuses on members' emotions, and even when noted for an individual, he addresses the entire group.

One of the central techniques of SCT is the application of the concept of the fork-in-the-road. As Agazarian has written:

> When we explain to ourselves and to others why we do what we do, we are using a map of the world and ourselves that we already know. Taking a journey to the inner self means exploring parts of ourselves we don't know ... Every time we come to a fork-in-the-road we need to choose the road to exploring and not the road to explaining. (1995/2010, p. 16)

The emphasis in exploring is to understand the entirety of the person's experience, not their explanation. Such a focus not only helps the person "relive" whatever they were trying to understand, but assists the clinician in gaining a better understanding of the person, which may then be shared, when appropriate, with the patient(s).

The overlap with Self Psychology is the focus on the individual's experience. The fork-in-the-road technique is closely allied with the two-part interpretative process outlined by Kohut (1977):

> First the analysand must realize that he has been understood; only then, as a second step, will the analyst demonstrate to the analysand the specific dynamic and genetic factors that explain the psychological content he had first empathically grasped. (p. 88)

Discussing the person's experience is different from inquiring about what the person is feeling or thinking. Often, or perhaps most often, patients do not know what they are feeling. They have been routinely asked that question by their therapist and, as a result, may sense the comment as a stereotyped intervention, and that the therapist is not really listening to understand. The Self-psychologically informed clinician tries to frame the intervention in a fashion that conveys efforts to understand the inner emotional state or the experience of the patient.

Example

A PD therapist might comment: "Anne, you have been talking about how you are anxious about visiting your family, who often seem to ignore you. This followed Beth's comment about how she directly confronted her husband and his behavior changed for the better. I wonder if you are trying to figure out how to do that with your family". The therapist might add, "Have I understood you correctly?"

Such an intervention indicates that the therapist is listening and trying to understand; he will share his understanding with the members and help them to reflect upon their inner experiences; that therapy is a collaborative process, not one in which the therapist makes a pronouncement. The intent is to help Anne examine her association as a response to Beth. Although Anne is speaking about the future, the therapist is drawing her attention to the likelihood that she is also resonating with Beth's experience with her husband. Moreover, he may be alluding to Beth, who, quite outside consciousness, initially told her story not only to share an accomplishment, but also to convey to Anne that she might become more assertive. The therapist, in his attention to the emotional ties between particular members, conveys this to the others so that they might reflect upon their experience of hearing Anne's response to Beth.

The SCT therapist might comment when Anne talks right after Beth's comment to her husband: "Anne, will you find out if Beth felt joined? If not, find out if the group is ready for a difference". This complex intervention has the potential for illuminating a number of principles of SCT. The intervention addresses Anne, which brings the discussion into the here-and-now (time boundary). It orients the group to functional subgrouping as the tool for building the group system for exploration. The intervention in an indirect manner asks all members to reflect upon what they have heard and what level of the communication they are "hearing", or "resonating with" in the SCT framework. It serves as a stimulus to further a therapeutic goal of increasing members' self-reflective, "observer-system" sensibilities. The SCT therapist calls this "working along", either actively in the subgroup or silently until they find enough resonance to join the subgroup. The functional subgrouping might be applicable at different levels: addressing anxiety or feeling strong and powerful. Work can take place in either of the subgroups.

The following example presents three segments (vignettes) from a single demonstration group that illustrate details of Self-psychological work, and how the demonstration group leader's understanding and intervening are conceptualized in Self Psychology and in SCT. The demonstration group was held in a fishbowl, with those who had not volunteered in a circle outside the group.

Example

Vignette 1

A woman comments that she feels like a baby and is looking to me for response (affirmation). I responded that she seemed to be putting herself down and I hoped that she could respond to me as an adult. Later in the session after a discussion of my injuring someone with my comment, the woman said that she felt that I had in a minor way hurt her. I responded: "good", by which I intended to convey that we were back working together and I had received her message that I had injured her.

Comment: As I reflected later on my initial intervention, I felt that it had been off the mark. My intention had been to help her accept childish feelings in relationship to me, but accept such feelings as part of what everyone, whether young or old, experiences. My theory was that we never outgrow childish feelings, but they remain a part of us, and that therapy can be helpful in accepting such inner responses rather than avoiding them in shame. Nevertheless, my direct "confrontation" that she was putting herself down was experienced by the woman as a put down, and unempathic. In response, she had withdrawn. When I understood this, I shared my understanding that I had injured her with the group. When she acknowledged that my comment was accurate, I commented, "good" (a mirroring response) with the intent of giving her recognition for her ability to self-reflect.

My intervention might be understood as an illustration of a counter-transference response to the greater context of the setting. I was experiencing a need to demonstrate aspects of Self Psychology, and I rather precipitously intervened to highlight the theoretical point about needing to accept childish feelings throughout one's life as an acceptable, but not too painful, shameful part of being human. Of course an alternative within the psychodynamic framework would have been to inquire more about the baby-like feelings she was having, but that was not an "option" under the counter-transferential pull of having to demonstrate my theory.

An SCT intervention would have delayed addressing the baby-like feelings and commented: "That's a frame. What can you say about what you're feeling/experiencing right now, and let's see if you have a subgroup". The intervention is gently inviting subgrouping. The subgrouping members would then discover together their experiences, moving beyond the frame of baby feelings. The potential for scapegoating the member with "baby" feelings would be diminished and members would be more willing to work with their own similar feelings.

In the post demonstration group discussion, participants explored a number of dynamic hypotheses regarding my interventions. Some participants saw my comments as infantilizing (by giving directions to feel like an adult) and giving a message that one should not talk about early experiences. My interventions were also signals that I might approve or disapprove of what they were doing, as exemplified by my comment, "good". However, others experienced my interventions as empathic and emphasizing growth.

A therapist can never be certain that his or her hoped for response from the patient will be forthcoming. Indeed, the recipient's experience of any intervention is what matters. In this first vignette the patient may experience the comment as either infantilizing or as an affirmation of work. Indeed, the further discussion of the experience helped me gain access to the counter-transferential basis for my initial intervention, and my task then was to accept what I had done.

Vignette 2

Part way through the session, following considerable discussion of how I had been leading the group, the same woman said that she would like to get to know others better and she would like it if the discussion stopped focusing on me. Her request seemingly was ignored as the members continued to focus on aspects of my leadership style. I then commented, wondering if the members were responding in a fashion that indicated that the request to shift to talking about member to member relationships was premature, and they were not ready to take that step. I also wondered if the woman had felt injured by the others' response. She acknowledged that she had felt frustrated, but that my response indicated that I was in tune with what was happening in the group and had understood what was happening with her, which had alleviated her distress.

Comment: In the post group discussion, my intervention was labeled an interpretation. I said that my intervention was intended to convey my understanding of what had happened. I differentiated understanding from "explaining" (an interpretation) which would include unconscious aspects of individuals or of the group process. The discussion highlighted how the use of the same term had different meanings for SCT and PD therapists and how these differences had the potential for leading to misunderstandings.

Vignette 3

In the latter part of the session a woman began coughing and she asked the observers to bring her some water. Her request was rather promptly met. I was startled, in one respect by the "audacity" of the request, the rapid response, and the apparent burst of energy within the group itself. I needed a few minutes to re-balance myself and try to sort out the possible meanings. During this interlude the members continued to focus on my leadership style. I provided another example, when I said that I thought that what had happened was a way to find out what kind of leader I was. My intention was to help the members step back from their excitement, reflect upon and verbalize their experience of the event.

Not surprisingly, a member commented that he had been waiting to see what I was going to do. I asked if others also were waiting for my response (similar to SCT's "Anyone else?"). Members then shared their various hopes and expectations of my leadership and my working towards the goal that I had set at the beginning of the session that volunteers would directly experience and about how a PD, self-psychologically oriented clinician works.

Comment: A PD therapist recognizes that trust has to be earned and safety tested. They are not achieved by pronouncement. Part of the process of group formation includes members trying to learn about the therapist and how he will respond to their expressions of emotions. These expressions, whether verbal or behavioral, are often experienced by the therapist as a test. In this vignette I did not initially understand the "message" the member might be sending because of my being slightly thrown off balance by the rapid action. When I "recovered" I was able to offer a possible understanding of what had transpired. My intervention was offered as a possible explanation, open to discussion and an invitation to explore alternative understandings of what had happened. I felt that a comment about boundaries or "acting" could lead members to processing the experience intellectually rather than reflect on their experiences during the episode. The SCT leader, recognizing that the request carried multiple possible meanings (authority/ boundary issues, creation of an identified patient), would ask the group to process the request, both for the requester and the members' impulses that were activated by the request.

Thinking about process

SCT and PD have found that psychic change requires a meaningful emotional experience in relationship to the group or its members. This process may occur within the relationship itself without having ever been brought fully to consciousness (Stern, et al., 1998) or through a combination of experience and cognitive processing. However, more complete and enduring results are achieved when a cognitive element is added to the experience. Both theories postulate a developmental sequence in which members reorganize the system and themselves in new and more effective ways of functioning.

Ornstein (2003) reviewed the concept of psychotherapeutic process and found a wide range of definitions in the literature. He surmised that these differences arose from the personal, the particular training, or the broader social system context. He notes that "the definition of the psychoanalytic process has to be open to accommodate the highly idiosyncratic, unique experiences of both participants in analysis" (pp. 19–20). Ornstein states "'Speaking about experiences' does not have the same transformative power as does 'speaking from within', with full emotional participation". (p. 22). Achieving this ability to speak from within, or in SCT terminology exploring one's experience instead of explaining it, is an important aspect of the therapeutic process.

Process then can be thought of as the movement within the therapy, whether moment to moment or over a broader perspective towards the therapeutic goal. This is not a linear movement, but is subject to many reversals, perturbations and derailments. Systems theory labels "processes" as those that address the system survival and development and those that address the relationship with the external environment (Agazarian, 1995/2010).

Both theories of group psychotherapy emphasize the importance of relationships that develop within the group as a major source of information about the individual in the pathway to change. This requires that members must learn how to trust and use the group to achieve that goal. Thus the therapist has a task of helping members begin to focus on the inner workings and to help them have experiences of and develop insight into the "behaviors" that facilitate growth and those that inhibit it; in SCT terms, driving and restraining forces.

The therapeutic process is seen to take place within the group. For both systems, the therapist's task is to begin to create and monitor boundaries so that work can take place both in the group and in relationship to the external world. The SCT therapists assist members' consolidation of theses processes by a final group agenda requesting members to consider "surprises, learnings, satisfactions, dissatisfactions and discoveries". The PD therapist hopes for the members to do that on their own, and without saying so directly, bring their ideas back to the meetings at later sessions.

One of the significant differences between PD and SCT processes is the therapist's use of authority in bringing the focus into the here-and-now. SCT therapists use their authority to provide instructions, i.e., "structuring", for how the therapy is to proceed. For example, the SCT therapist asks the members to focus on being present in the group. Similarly, noting when members cross boundaries, (e.g., "you are talking about the past, the future, or you are predicting events in the future") is a way of helping members focus on their experience in the here-and-now.

The goal of the dynamic therapist is similar, but accomplished in a different manner. The PD clinician generally focuses on members' anxiety in exploring experiences in the here-and-now. If the group seems to be in flight, the PD therapist has several options within the theoretical framework. An intervention may be directed to the individual who seems to be responding to the anxiety of the situation through flight behavior or by speaking metaphorically. Both elements were apparent in the example of Anne and Beth above. In that illustration, the therapist attempted to bring his understanding of Anne's association to her forthcoming visit as linked to Beth's description of her successful confrontation with her husband. The intervention might be directed to the group-as-a-whole, observing the possibility that the members have accepted the shift in topic to protect themselves from the discomfort of the topic; the therapist might add the anxiety associated with being assertive. This would be similar to an SCT comment that the member displaying flight behavior seems to be a voice for the group.

The level of individual and group development influences members' ability to utilize group-as-a-whole interventions. Experience has shown that unless they are properly timed, such group-as-a-whole interpretations are likely to have a deleterious effect on the group. Horwitz (1977) noted that without evidence of a therapeutic alliance, interpretations are rejected or responded to aversively. Stone (2005), writing from a self psychological framework, comments that the therapist must be alert to any group-as-a-whole intervention as being experienced by one or more members as off the mark and as a narcissistic injury. Stern (2009), working in dyadic setting, states: "The non-linear, unpredictable, ever-changing nature of the intersubjective interaction, which requires a kind of openness and freedom on the part of the analyst as he attempts to keep up and register all that is going on at 'the cutting-edge' of the interaction and his moment-to-moment experience and understanding of the patient" (p. 151). The group therapist has a much more difficult task of following the process, but must remain ever alert to the potential for injury (Stone, 2001).

SCT therapists also would not make group-as-a-whole interpretations until the group had achieved an appropriate phase of development. Every system develops by splitting into differences and integrating them (Agazarian, 1995/2010). When functional subgrouping has been well established members would be able to work with and integrate differences if a group-as-a-whole intervention had been responded to with different emotions. If this response did not occur, the SCT therapist might well notice an injury that was not recognized by the members, comment on it, and ask for members to subgroup with the prominent emotion.

Some additional process observations

I have been observing Yvonne for more than two decades as she began to apply her systems concepts. I watched her work with volunteers as she demonstrated the concepts in demonstration groups, primarily at the American Group Psychotherapy Association (AGPA) conferences, once during a special weekend in New York, and most recently during two annual conferences held by the Systems-Centered Training and Research Institute. As I recall in the early period, the most striking aspect of the experiences was the attendees' willingness to participate in a group that exposed them to a markedly different experience than the then dominant psychodynamic/analytic orientation.

My personal experience in participating in an SCT demonstration group more than 20 years ago was of being controlled and dominated by Yvonne's presence. The experience was one of being in a group that was frequently interrupted with another instruction on how to behave. It seemed like almost in mid-sentence Yvonne would ask, "Who would like to join the subgroup of ...?" I do not recall the precise words, but it felt very much like a demand. The group seemed to split, with those who overtly complied and those who rather angrily rebelled, usually silently. When she was challenged, Yvonne was clear and firm about her efforts to demonstrate the value of subgrouping. Part of this made a great deal of sense—the experience of not being alone, and being clear that someone else shared my emotions, certainly felt very important. I had no trouble recognizing how that would facilitate group development, and how it would allow members to more readily become engaged in examining differences, rather than being dismissive or angry with the other person, or subgroup. Nevertheless, the overriding experience of the time was one of feeling that this was not really therapy, as I knew it. I felt that the member's iatrogenic induced anger was ignored, and Yvonne plowed ahead. I also knew that the anger must have been worked with in some fashion, but I was not privileged to see the process by which that took place because of the time-limited nature of the demonstration group.

Fast-forward twenty years. In 2008 I observed Yvonne work at an AGPA conference with people who seemed relatively unfamiliar with her work. What was so striking was that I did not experience anger, as I had in the past. To the best of my observational ability, neither did the participants. I suddenly realized that Yvonne's accumulated experience and greater comfort with her theory seemed to have produced a subtle but palpable difference in the tone and style with which she made interventions. They seemed very similar to what I had observed in the past, yet the response was so strikingly different. I believe that the change in the members' response may have included a greater willingness to learn and a greater acceptance of the SCT model, but I believe the calmer response was in the relational tone of Yvonne's intervention. The group atmosphere was co-constructed.

Of course this should not be a great surprise when one thinks about the response to new ideas or ways of doing things. Almost invariably, there is a period of doubt accompanied by hostility of varying intensity. As the value of the new ideas is understood they become integrated into the mainstream, and at times even subverted with comments such as, "nothing new was added". I don't believe that such will be the case with SCT because it has developed a distinctive vocabulary, but many of the ideas are useful to more traditional clinicians.

I hope that that the readers of this contribution, whether oriented to SCT or to PD, can learn from the few illustrations I have presented. To do so would be a fitting honor of Yvonne and her work.

Acknowledgement

The author wishes to thank Susan Gantt and Mark Johnson who graciously assisted me in preparation of this manuscript.

References

Agazarian, Y. M. (1995/2010). Five papers from the Friends Hospital training series: Fall 1992—Fall 1995. In Carter, F. Lum, K. Peightel, J. Robbins, M. Silverstein, M. Vadell, J. Viskari, S. E. (Eds.), *Systems-centered theory and practice: The contribution of Yvonne Agazarian* (pp. 1–46). Livermore, CA: WingSpan Press. (Previously unpublished papers)

Horwitz, L. (1977). A group-centered approach to group psychotherapy. *International Journal of Group Psychotherapy, 27*, 423–439.

Kohut, H. (1977). *The restoration of the self.* New York: International Universities Press.

Ornstein, P. H. (2003). The elusive concept of the psychoanalytic process. *Journal of the American Psychoanalytic Association, 52*, 15–41.

Stern, D. N., Sander, L. W., Nahrum, J. P., Harrison, A. M., Lyons-Ruth, K., Morgan, A. C., Bruschweiler-Stern, N. & Tronick, E. Z. (1998). The process change study group. Non-interpretive mechanisms in psychoanalytic therapy: The "something more" than interpretation. *The International Journal of Psychoanalysis, 79*, 903–921.

Stern, S. (2009). The dialectic of empathy and freedom. *International Journal of Psychoanalytic Self Psychology, 4*, 132–164.

Stone, W. N. (2001). The role of the therapist's affect in the detection of empathic failures, misunderstandings and injury. *Group: The Journal of the Eastern Group Psychotherapy Society, 25*, 3–14.

Stone, W. N. (2005). Group-as-a-whole: A self psychological perspective. *Group: The Journal of the Eastern Group Psychotherapy Society, 29*, 239–255.

INDEX